Emotional Regulation Skills for Kids

A Guide for Parents to Develop Emotional Connection, Nurture Positive Behavior, Relationship and Communicate Effectively with Children aged 3-10

By

Fruitful Publishers

© **Copyright 2023 by Fruitful Publishers - All rights reserved.**

Without the prior written permission of the Publisher, no part of this publication may be stored in a retrieval system, replicated, or transferred in any form or medium, digital, scanning, recording, printing, mechanical, or otherwise, except as permitted under UK Copyright Act and 1976 United States Copyright Act, section 107 or 108. Permission concerns should be directed to the publisher's permission department.

Legal Notice

This book is copyright protected. It is only to be used for personal purposes. Without the author's or publisher's permission, you cannot paraphrase, quote, copy, distribute, sell, or change any part of the information in this book.

Disclaimer Notice

This book is written and published independently. Please keep in mind that the material in this publication is solely for educational and entertaining purposes. All efforts have provided authentic, up-to-date, trustworthy, and comprehensive information. There are no express or implied assurances. The purpose of this book's material is to assist readers in having a better understanding of the subject matter. The activities, information, and exercises are provided solely for self-help information. This book is not intended to replace expert psychologists, legal, financial, or other guidance. If you require counseling, please get in touch with a qualified professional. By reading this text, the reader accepts that the author will not be held liable for any damages, indirectly or directly, experienced due to the use of the information included herein, particularly, but not limited to, omissions, errors, or inaccuracies. As a reader, you are accountable for your decisions, actions, and consequences.

Table of Contents

INTRODUCTION 5

CHAPTER 1 7

WHY KIDS STRUGGLE WITH PROBLEM BEHAVIOR? 7
- 1.1 Tantrums can be a Learned Behavior 8
- 1.2 Cope with your Child's Negative Feelings 9
- 1.3 Helping Kids Cope with Negative Feelings 13
- 1.4 Five Ways to Handle Negative Emotions in Your Child 21

CHAPTER 2 24

EXPRESS YOUR STRONG FEELINGS WITHOUT BEING HURTFUL 24
- 2.1 Tips for Maintaining a Confident, Constructive Outlook 24
- 2.2 Why Transitions Trigger Problem Behavior 28
- 2.3 After the Time Out 32

CHAPTER 3 35

HELPING KIDS DEAL WITH EMOTIONS 35
- 3.1 Developing Emotional IQ 35
- 3.2 Medication 42
- 3.3 Do Babies Feel Empathy? 45

CHAPTER 4 51

EMOTION COACHING AND TIPS FOR PARENTS 51
- 4.1 Tips for Being a Better Emotion Coach 51
  - (4.1.1) *Twelve evidence-based Tips for making Life Better* 51
  - (4.1.2) *Twelve evidence-based suggestions for dealing with Anger, Resistance, and Acting out in Disruptive Behavior Problems* 57
  - (4.1.3) *Ten Substitutes for Spanking* 68
- 4.2 Take Advantage of Every Opportunity to Talk about your Feelings and the Conditions that Cause Them 70
  - (4.2.1) *Don't minimize or dismiss your Child's sentiments, and don't penalize him/her for expressing Negative Emotions* 81
- 4.3. Alternative Solutions for your Child when He/She is Upset or Sad 81
  - (4.3.1) *Twelve evidence-based strategies for assisting children in making friends* 82

(4.3.2) Children's facial expressions: Assisting them in Reading Emotions 92
(4.3.3) What can we do to assist children in Reading Faces? 95
4.4 INSTILL A POSITIVE, CONSTRUCTIVE ATTITUDE 98

CHAPTER 5 104

AUTHORITARIAN PARENTING 104

5.1 WHAT HAPPENS TO CHILDREN WHEN THEIR PARENTS ARE AUTHORITARIAN? 104
5.2 EMOTIONAL ISSUES...108
5.3 SET TOUGH BOUNDARIES WHILE MAINTAINING GOODWILL 112

CONCLUSION 115

USEFUL TIPS FOR PARENTS AND GUARDIANS 115
ASPECT OF SPIRIT, SOUL AND BODY 119

THANKS GIVING NOTE 120

Introduction

'Emotional Regulation Skills for Kids' is a guide for communication between parents or teachers and kids. It includes fresh insights, suggestions and methods to solve common problems and build foundations for lasting relationships. Complete with age-appropriate strategies for dealing with day-to-day struggles that will help you explain these concepts to your child, it shows you how to cultivate healthy, emotional and intellectual development so that your kids can lead balanced, meaningful, and connected lives. This breakthrough book demonstrates how parents and teachers can join forces to inspire kids to be self-directed, self-disciplined, and responsive to the wonders of learning.

'Emotional Regulation Skills for Kids' will help parents from all walks of life to raise the happiest, most well-adjusted kids in the world.

According to a recent study, more than 70% of parents admit they "struggle" to have meaningful conversations with their children. It should be simple to communicate with your children, yet miscommunication is simpler. The longer you put off having a genuine conversation with your children, the worse it will get over time. You know in your heart that there is no time to waste and that your circumstances need to alter right away. Once you understand the concepts in this book, you'll discover that parenting may be more enjoyable. Healthy communication is essential for raising children with self-esteem and respect for one another, whether they are toddlers or teenagers.

'Emotional Regulation Skills for Kids' illustrates the remarkable relationship between a child's development and the way a parent responds to misbehavior. It shows you how to deal with temper tantrums, fights, and tears without making a big deal out of them. The writer defines the fundamental purpose of this book — to instruct, not to yell at or chastise — and then goes on to explain how to communicate with your child, manage emotions, and convert a meltdown into a chance for learning.

When you do this, solving a problem becomes a win-win situation, which stops the cycle of bad behavior (and punishment).

Effective communication is essential to healthy parenting. The issue is that, as parents, we rarely communicate. This is not only unproductive, but it also deters kids from speaking their hearts. The author provides the greatest listening techniques to improve family connections and prepare your kids for success in this incredibly useful book. Intentional talking and listening will provide your child, whether they are in preschool, elementary school, or high school, the confidence they need to establish their own voice. When you're older, your current habits will help you keep in touch with people for a long time.

Your communication style with your children can have a profound impact on their lives. However, let's say you find it difficult to speak with your kids. You don't have to worry about that anymore since this book, '**Emotional Regulation Skills for Kids**,' has precise, easy-to-use strategies for improving communication with your children.

Our Goal

Our goal is to give ideas and guidance to parents and teachers to get all parts of a healthy child's brain working together.

Hold your seat, lets drive to the first chapter of this amazing book.

Chapter 1

Why Kids Struggle With Problem Behavior?

When kids experience frequent emotional outbursts, it may indicate that they haven't yet mastered the abilities to cope with emotions such as irritation, worry, or wrath. Managing strong emotions in a healthy and adult manner necessitates a number of abilities, including:

- Emotional self-regulation
- Impulse control
- Problem solving
- Negotiating
- Delaying gratification
- Knowing what's appropriate or expected in a given situation
- Communicating wishes and needs to adults

Other kids may appear to have a harder time setting boundaries and adhering to rules. They may be stubborn, disobey orders, or try to persuade themselves out of doing things that aren't voluntary.

You may notice patterns of behavior that appear at specific times of the day (such as night), during specific tasks (such as homework), or with specific persons. You may also notice that your child misbehaves more at home than at school or that he/she acts up more at school than at home. Tantrums and other forms of outbursts are a common and even beneficial aspect of growing up. They're signs that a kid is growing up — signs that he or she is pushing limits, gaining skills and views, and learning about the world around them. However, when a kid acts out frequently, it can strain the parent-child bond, causing recurrent frustration and resentment in the family that isn't good. This guide is designed to explain more about how kids learn to manage their behavior, what parents can do to help, and how to get more support if you need it, whether your kid is at the beginning of learning about self-regulation and limitations or if your family has been starting to struggle and you are looking for help.

1.1 Tantrums can be a Learned Behavior

Tantrums and other instances of inappropriate conduct are sometimes perceived as planned or manipulative by parents. Tantrums are normally not a choice behavior on the side of a child, but they may be what is known as a "learned behavior," according to clinicians who specialize in kids' behavior. This means that kids learn that throwing a tantrum will get them what they desire.

To put it another way, a child who struggles to control his/her emotions may not be deliberately planning his/her tantrums, but he/she may be resorting to them because he/she hasn't learned a better approach to solve problems or communicate his/her demands. Well-intentioned parents frequently respond to tantrums by attempting to resolve the issue – by consoling the kid or providing his/her with whatever he/she is requesting. Unfortunately, this promotes tantrum behavior, making kids more likely to have tantrums in the future and less likely to learn more sophisticated ways of managing their emotions.

Responding to Problem Behavior

When their kids act out, parents frequently feel helpless. You may have tried a variety of disciplinary strategies without much success. In fact, trying too many different tactics for dealing with disruptive behavior can be part of the problem because kids react better to continuous reinforcement of clear boundaries. But don't get disheartened if you haven't noticed any progress yet; parents have more power than they realize when their kids are acting defiantly. You can start to change kids' conduct and even the parent-child connection by employing tactics advised by child mental health specialists who have expertise in behavior management. This section starts with some general guidelines that behavior experts offer as helpful ways for dealing with troublesome behavior in the present. It then delves deeper into the problem behavior, which can be useful for parents who want to learn more about why their kids misbehave and how to address specific behaviors they wish to alter.

1.2 Cope with your Child's Negative Feelings

Negative Feelings, Essential Signals on the Road of Life: Supporting our Kids on their Path

While dealing with our own pain is difficult enough, witnessing our kids struggle may be nearly impossible! It's normal to want to ignore things that make us feel very uncomfortable or unhappy, especially if we're attempting to protect our kids from them. And it goes without saying that suffering over extended periods of time is intolerable. But the truth is that life is not without pain, both bodily and emotional.

Our kids must be able to breathe independently and indicate their distress from the minute they are born. And as parents, it is our responsibility to assist kids in coping with their discomfort so that they can learn to care for themselves. Understanding negative feelings and what they signify might help our kids pay attention to important information and navigate their lives more efficiently. In today's world, our kids have a plethora of options for avoiding and escaping unwanted feelings and discomfort. They have instant access to sources of distractions and amusement at the tip of their hands.

They can take mom's phone from her purse at practically any time, so they don't have to wait in the grocery line or, worse, we offer it to them, so they remain quiet during meals at the restaurant. Instead of waiting for something innovative to arise during unstructured time, kids can quickly fill the void by playing tablet games. They can check social media, read tweets, or send selfies when they first feel lonely. They don't even have to put up with TV advertisements or listen to a piece of odd music because their broadcasts have been recorded, and their own playlists have been created.

Meal delivery services, fast food places, and precooked boxed meals all reinforce the premise that everything should be fast, simple, and to their liking, avoiding the "inconvenience" of shopping, cooking, and cleaning it up.

All of this is in addition to the learning they receive from adults who use liquor or illegal drugs to deal with their own negative emotions. Even though pharmaceuticals might be beneficial, expecting them to alleviate all discomfort sends a message to our kids that any discomfort is inappropriate and unpleasant.

Avoiding or escaping negative emotions removes the very challenge that breeds inspiration, fortitude, bravery and growth, limiting our kids's access to their full potential.

This raises the question of what our kids are missing out on by avoiding these sentiments. What is the indication that each bad feeling is sending?

Let's take a look at a few of them and see what we can learn from them. Anger and fear, for example, serve a protective purpose. They're reactions to danger and unfairness.

- **Fear**, a natural reaction to an imminent disaster, causes us to hit the brakes and seek a proactive defensive response. In reaction to a sensation of anxiety, planning, strategy, preparation, hard work, finding resources, and asking for aid can all be mobilized. Personal safety necessitates the expression of unpleasant emotions. They are part of the scratches and bruises that come with being human, and they help to create tolerance, empathy, and experience in order to face future obstacles.

- **Anger** awakens the desire to put an end to something or face injustice in order to effect change. Our kids must be able to successfully deal with threats to their safety, protect themselves, and channel their rage into positive change. Anger can help kids exert authority, speak up, and advocate for a better future as they grow older.

- **Sadness** alerts us to the fact that we have suffered a loss. It could be the end of a relationship or a dream, a sensation of helplessness, or an unfulfilled expectation.

This emotion can elicit sympathy from others and prompt introspection, allowing us to ponder how we can improve. Being able to recover back from disappointments or failures can help you develop the judgment you'll need on the next challenge.

- **Embarrassment** indicates that they acted in a way that was not socially acceptable, signaling that they should examine their future conduct. Embarrassment, remorse, envy, and jealousy are all termed "social emotions," and their purpose is to help our kids think about how they fit in with others so they may make modifications to keep their relationships. And that's why it is particularly difficult throughout the adolescent years when to fit in is so important.

- **Disgust** is essential for disease prevention and cleanliness.

- **Guilt**, on the other hand, informs them that they have transgressed their own moral code. When we harm or insult someone, the agony of this unpleasant emotion promotes an apology and mending. Guilt also teaches our kids to control their emotions to act on their wishes when doing so could insult or damage others.

- When accepted as knowledge, the distress caused by these social emotions can urge change in order to fit in socially. Envy and jealousy, on the other hand, are comparing emotions.

- When our kids compare themselves to another and think that they are weaker in some way, they experience envy. This discomfort can help your kid distinguish his/her own uniqueness and discover his/her distinctive gifts.

- **Jealousy** is the fear of losing a significant relationship. The agony of this emotion reveals crucial information about the type of person we need and what it takes to maintain a relationship going.

Fitting in and forming relationships are important aspects of living a full life, and these bad social feelings assist our kids in learning how to do so. While we all have a lot of diversions and conveniences in our life that make us numb to our emotions, it's important to think about how this avoidance affects our kids. The ability to swiftly avoid or flee discomfort may impair our kids in a way that is comparable to driving blind. Negative emotions provide us with crucial knowledge. In the face of danger, fear acts like a stop sign or an orange traffic signal, warning us to proceed with caution or reevaluate our actions. Uncontrolled rage is like driving a powerful sports vehicle carelessly, leaving a trail of destruction in its wake. Harnessed rage, on the other hand, is productive, resulting in new signs being placed, potholes being repaired, and laws being amended. Keeping with the metaphor, grief helps us accept what is and stimulates us to think about how we might find alternative routes in the future.

To be able to share the road while following the laws to drive safely, we must bear the social feelings of shame, guilt, envy, and jealousy.

All of these emotions are like traffic lights, turn signals, white, yellow, single, and double painted lines on the road, speed bumps and restrictions, highway and street signs that guide us safely from point A to point B.

When we hand our kids a tablet to avoid a tantrum in the restaurant or use our phone to occupy their boredom in the grocery queue, it's crucial for us, as parents, to adopt a different approach to their bad sentiments. Rather than escaping or avoiding them, we must assist our kids in confronting their negative emotions and learning from them. Why don't you unplug the devices?

Cooking together and making dinner a time for catching up on the day's events can be a fun way to spend time together. Allow your kids to hear about how you overcame and grew from your negative emotions. Encourage them to talk about their own. Validate how inconvenient it is to be humiliated, unhappy, afraid, or guilty, and demonstrate that you understand. Weep with them and give them hugs.

You can also demonstrate how to apologize and make amends. Overall, rather than viewing unpleasant emotions as something to be avoided, consider them as necessary for our kids to learn how to navigate their life path. While no parent likes to see their child suffer, we must accept that suffering is an inevitable part of life. Avoiding or escaping negative emotions can be an obstacle that we need to assist our kids to overcome in order for them to realize their full potential.

1.3 Helping Kids Cope with Negative Feelings

Emotion coaching is the process of communicating with kids regarding their feelings and providing them with coping methods for emotionally challenging situations. It's important to empathize, reassure, and educate.

Is there any difference?

Yes. Here's a look at the research and some pointers on how to become a better emotion coach.

Tuning in: Why kids need emotional support

They physically may be little, but their emotional reactions are anything but. Young kids are exposed to a variety of disappointments and sources of negativity. Anger, despair, anxiety, and fear are common emotions they experience.

What are our options?

Kids are, without a doubt, works in progress. We shouldn't expect a 3-year-old kid to handle disappointment in the same manner that a 30-year-old does since parts of the brain that specialize in self-regulation are still growing.

Furthermore, young kids do not have the same life experiences as us. They're only just starting to understand how emotions function. They aren't as good at interpreting other people's emotions and motives.

They require learning and practice opportunities. Some kids have it more difficult than others. Certain personality qualities are rather stable over time, while others, such as moodiness, anger, anxiety, or sadness, put you at higher risk for emotional issues. That isn't to say that kids can't progress. Even small kids can learn to better control their emotions. They simply require our assistance. It's up to us to make sure we give it.

Dismissing, disapproving, and ignoring

When your kid is upset, how do you generally respond? Several common patterns have been observed.

Parents may dismiss their kids's unpleasant emotions in some instances. They convey the impression that sentiments are trivial or insignificant. On other occasions, parents have expressed their disapproval. They are aware of their kids' emotions but find negative emotion displays disrespectful. And, while some parents recognize and accept their kids' unpleasant emotions, they make no attempt to assist them. They frequently regard unpleasant feelings, such as melancholy, as "something to get over, ride out, but not concentrate on. They may wish there was more they could do, but they have no idea what that something is.

Parents who disregard, disapprove or avoid their kids aren't necessarily insensitive to them. They may, on the other hand, find it distressing to see their kids in anguish. However, they fail to teach kids how to deal with internal emotional storms.

Instead, they sit on the sidelines or use taunting, threats, or punishment to try to control their emotions. They might, for example, react to a child's rage by imposing a "time out" - even if the kid has done nothing wrong.

Emotion coaching represents a very different approach

Emotion coaching parents see their kids's negative moods as possibilities to sympathize, connect, and teach their kids. They take the time to understand and appreciate the kid by seeing things from his/her point of view.

They discuss emotions with kids and assist them in expressing their own sentiments. They also assist kids in developing skills for dealing with negative emotions and the circumstances that cause them.

What's the evidence that emotion coaching works?

Emotion coaching has been linked to better child outcomes in observational studies. Kids who receive coaching have fewer emotional and behavioral issues, such as anger, anxiety, and acting out. They have greater social skills and peer relationships as well.

Do correlations like this indicate causation? Certainly not. It's possible that well-behaved, socially skilled kids encourage parents to chat with them about emotional concerns.

There is experimental evidence. When kids with behavioral issues are taught how to be better emotion coaches by their parents, the kids' behavior improves.

Even a simple reminder can have an impact. Researchers spent only 15 minutes reinforcing parents' emotion coaching methods in a preschool study. They next watched as the parents engaged with their kids while completing a difficult activity. Parents showed more emotional sensitivity and good humor after the intervention, while their kids responded to frustrating experiences with more tenacity and excitement.

Not a magic cure-all

Of course, emotion counseling isn't a panacea for all issues. Some kids have issues that require more than just emotional training to resolve.

However, it is obvious that empathy, sensitive communication, and intelligent problem-solving aid in the development of emotional competence in kids. Here's how to do it well, based on research. There are some students with whom teachers do not share the same feelings as the rest of their students. In reality, some students may be openly disliked by their teachers.

This is a common occurrence. But what can a teacher do in such a situation? What options does he/she have for dealing with this situation?

In search of explanations

A teacher can ask himself/herself several key questions to help his/her better understand why he/she feels the way he/she does.

- Does the child's demeanor reflect someone with whom he/she is uncomfortable, with whom he/she has had a falling out, or with whom he/she has been harmed in some way?

- Is there something about the child's physical appearance or behavior that bothers her?

- Teachers can influence a child's behavior by altering how he/she thinks about his/her actions. They must, however, adjust their mindsets when it comes to more subtle, even subconscious characteristics like habits and appearance.

- How can a teacher modify the way he/she thinks about those things he/she can't change, such as his/her mannerisms, appearance, or other physical characteristics? The first step is to become aware of the problem.

The following are some questions he/she can ask himself/herself:

- Is there someone I know or have known in the past who has the same mannerisms as this child?

- Is there anything about that individual that makes me uncomfortable (a falling out, he/she wounded me)?

- Does this kid remind me of aspects of myself that I dislike?

- The underlying causes of his/her feelings can provide new insight into his/her relationships with this kid if they can be identified. The teacher can now move on to the next level by confronting his/her feelings.

- Concentrate on the good aspects of the child and how he/she is special.

- Make a concerted effort to give this kid the same amount of attention as other kids.

- Act in ways that make the kid feel competent and confident in himself/herself.

- With time, the teacher may develop a favorable attitude toward the child as a result of his/her new insights, which may allow his/her to see the kid in a whole new light.

Disruptive behaviors

A child's behavior might sometimes be the source of a problem. Because he makes it tough to teach, a disruptive kid may be difficult to like. Bullies, teasers, and people who inflict emotional harm on others are all guilty of this.

When teachers report kids's behavior to their parents, put them to time out, or otherwise discipline them, the kids get more enraged and frustrated and are more inclined to express their sentiments in ways that enrage and frustrate their teachers and peers. Even when accompanied by reasons ("You won't have any friends if you act that way."), telling kids what to do and what not to do sometimes falls on deaf ears. The instructor is irritated by this point, and the psychological barrier between him/her and the kid is widening. A teacher must recognize that these kids's personal needs are not being satisfied for whatever reason. Many of these kids believe that disrupting or damaging activities will give them power, garnering respect and, eventually, the friendship of people who shun them, whether they are bullied at home or otherwise insecure.

Kids who do not have their basic needs satisfied may develop apathy toward themselves and disruption becomes their coping mechanism. And kids who are just concerned with themselves are incapable of caring for others.

What you can do

What can a teacher do to assist these kids in developing empathy, a trait that will help them care about others and help them care about themselves?

First and foremost, kids should be empowered rather than overpowered. Instead of our teaching them what they should and should not do and why kids can learn to tell us what they should and should not do and why starting as early as age four.

Instead of focusing solely on the behavior, including the child in the discourse to encourage him/her to consider what he/she is doing by asking questions like:

- What will happen if you scream at (or kick) a classmate?

- What would you think if something happened to you?

- What do you think I (or he/she) might be thinking?

- What can you do to stop this from happening?

These types of questions help people empathize with one another. "I might make you furious" or "I might hurt him/her" are common responses from kids. Punishment and threats may temporarily stop a behavior, but they originate from the outside. Kids who consider their own and others' feelings are less likely to do harm to themselves or others. That is something that comes from within. We must first show kids that we care about them if we want them to care about others. With a child we don't like, that can be challenging. However, if these kids learn to care about themselves, they will recognize that others, including their teachers, have feelings as well. As a result, teachers may begin to have positive feelings about them.

Frustration and Anger

Taming aggression in children: 5 strategies for effective parenting

Angry tantrums, striking, kicking, or biting; hot-headed outbursts that destroy property; cool-headed bullying; verbal attacks; attempts to dominate others by threats or violence are all examples of kid aggression.

What causes kids to become agitated?

Kids may lash out because they are frustrated by an issue that is too big for them to handle. They haven't sorted out how to deal with their emotions or resolve problems in a socially acceptable manner.

In other circumstances, kids may be dealing with unique challenges, such as traumatic life events, emotional regulation issues, attention impairments, autism signs, or hyperactivity. Adults can have a tremendous influence in all cases, even when kids have been diagnosed with major behavior disorders. We aren't programmed to respond to the world with hostility; thus, aggression doesn't happen. We are all capable of acting aggressively. Whether or not we do so is determined by how we view the world.

Kids's aggressive dispositions are formed by their environment — the pressures, risks, opportunities, and consequences they face. We can improve behavior and affect the course of development by adjusting these settings. That isn't to say it's your fault if your child is misbehaving.

Some kids are at a higher risk of getting into trouble due to genetic factors. Early life stress has the same effect.

Genes put some of us at a higher risk for aggressive conduct, according to large-scale twin research. And youngsters who are exposed to a lot of stress early in life are more prone to develop aggressive behavior problems.

Kids's aggression is influenced by factors outside the family as well.

Peers, instructors, neighborhoods, messages in the media, beliefs, and cultural elements all play a part. These environmental effects will differ based on your child's DNA, prenatal circumstances, and early life stress exposure.

According to studies, some kids do not respond to stressful conditions with a normal surge in the stress hormone cortisol. Others may have a spike, but it takes an extremely long period for them to recover. Both types of youngsters are more likely to develop aggressive behavior issues.

However, whatever variables put a child in danger, the outcome is not predetermined. Caregivers who receive the assistance they require can have a significant influence. When parents receive practical training and moral support, aggressive kids's behavior changes, according to randomized, controlled studies.

Parents learn specialized methods for dealing with violence, which helps the interventions work. They work, however, because parents learn to modify their perspectives. It's frustrating and depressing to deal with a child's behavioral issues. It depletes your willpower, optimism, competence, and goodwill. It has the potential to destabilize the parent-child relationship by causing you to think about your kid in ways that are detrimental to your capacity to cope.

Negative thoughts exacerbate conflict and exacerbate behavioral issues. You can prevent harmful conduct from erupting if you replace these toxic mental patterns with positive, productive, problem-solving thinking.

So, whether our kids are going through the "terrible twos" or are dealing with more serious issues, we should be encouraged. We can change things if we have the correct tools. Here are two portions of evidence-based advice for dealing with kids's hostility. The first section is about changing your perspective as a parent.

1.4 Five Ways to Handle Negative Emotions in Your Child

As parents, we don't want this situation that our kids suffer, so we try to shield them from negative feelings like annoyance, irritation, failure, grief, and disappointment. However, we send some dangerous messages when we rush to erase barriers from their path or soothe away their distress too quickly:

We're saying we don't think they'll be able to handle what the world throws at them, that they are not able to control their own emotions, which can become a self-fulfilling prophecy.

We're also implying that we believe bad feelings should be avoided at all costs, encouraging our kids to stuff them down.

Negative emotions do not go away, according to researchers, but rather return in ever more violent forms, as most current psychologists concur. Emotions must be expressed before they may be released.

Indeed, many psychologists regard the ability to express negative emotions in a healthy manner as a pillar of mental health. And this is something that our kids can do from the moment they are born.

The only healthy method to feel better when we're depressed is to move through a bad emotion or to "ride the wave," as it were. Rather than stuffing the emotion, sit with it, accept it, and learn from it. But it may be so tempting to deny our kids' less-than-happy states when we have such a concentrated agenda on their pleasure. So, what can we do to assist them in working through their feelings and emerging healthy on the other side?

First, regulate yourself

If negative feelings elicit a strong reaction in you, consider it an opportunity to sort them out. Were there any emotions that were not tolerated in your childhood? Was sobbing turned off?

Was disappointment proven to be unfounded? Was there a muffled uproar? If that's the case, do some introspection and consider which "shoulds" you're clinging to. It might be time to set them free.

You won't be able to hold a safe place for your child to get through their huge unpleasant feelings if you are provoked by them.

Cultivate a detached empathy

You need to get to a position where you can hold space for them without being overly involved in their emotions. If you identify too strongly with their feelings, you will become entangled with them and will be unable to provide the stability they require.

Imagine them like a ship in a storm; they require a calm, level-headed captain who isn't fazed by storms.

Furthermore, when you combine your strong emotions with theirs, you overwhelm their ability to self-regulate. Saying comments like "It makes Mommy sad when you're sad" just adds to their already difficult emotions of guilt and stress. They need to know that you're alright, albeit sympathetic, regardless of how they're feeling.

Accept emotions — not behaviors

On the one hand, we strive to be emotionally tolerant, to validate and empathize with our kids' difficult feelings, but it is also our responsibility to keep them and others safe. If their actions are violent, destructive, regretful, or cruel, you may need to set boundaries for them while empathizing with the feelings that motivate them.

For example, you might ask your kid to stop weeping or fussing, keep their hands to themselves, or return anything they've grabbed, yet you still empathize with their distress.

Develop your child's emotional vocabulary

Take the chance to name the emotion they're feeling and provide them terminology to express it safely.

The more clearly you and your kid can explain the emotion, the simpler it will be for you and your kid to feel "heard" and get past it.

Provide a healthy outlet

Your kid might not know how to communicate their sadness, shame, or despair in a healthy way.

Allow them to express themselves through art, dance, painting, or singing; any creative outlet can be incredibly restorative. Playing out feelings with dolls or puppets may, of course, be a great release for kids. Are you affected by your child's bad emotions? How do you assist them, as well as yourself, in moving through them?

Chapter 2

Express your Strong Feelings Without Being Hurtful

2.1 Tips for Maintaining a Confident, Constructive Outlook

1. Don't take it personally

It's easy to feel disrespected when your kid refuses to comply with a request. When your kid flies into a rage, it's easy to feel targeted. However, these natural emotional reactions are incorrect.

For starters, kids do not process emotions and information in the same manner that adults do. There's a lot your kid doesn't comprehend about his/her own feelings, let alone yours if he/she's young. Even if your kids are older, his/her misbehavior is most likely due to impulsivity or incompetence, not malice.

Second, research reveals that our negative social views — the inclination to impute hostile intents to those who don't have them — might become self-fulfilling. People who expect the worst are more likely to generate negative responses from others. Parents who assign antagonistic motives to their kids may end up exacerbating the very problems they are trying to remedy.

In one study, mothers who made hostile attributions about their toddlers were more likely to have kids with aggressive behavior problems three and a half years later.

Even after the researchers adjusted for pre-existing kid issues and the bad parenting behavior that often goes along with hostile attributions, the association between maternal opinions and kid aggression remained substantial.

It's not simply helpful for your attitude to remind yourself not to take things personally. It is beneficial to both your relationship and your kid's long-term growth.

2. Get realistic expectations about your kid's ability to follow rules and comply with requests

Young kid's memory spans are shorter, and they are quickly distracted. Verbal instructions take longer for them to process. Their working memory capacity — the total amount of things they can remember at any given time — is more constrained.

It may take more time than anticipated to learn new material or adjust to a change in rules or practice. Young kids, on the other hand, require more practice than older kids, while older kids require more practice than adults.

As a result, we shouldn't expect young toddlers to respond fast and efficiently when we give them instructions. They work at a slower pace and have a more difficult time transitioning from one activity to the next. They require clear, uncomplicated instructions from us, as well as the extra time they require to switch gears.

Although older kids are capable of handling greater complexity and speed, their attention spans, working memory capabilities, impulse control, and task-switching abilities are still developing. By paying attention to your kid's pace and ability, as well as providing patient, calm reminders, you can modify the assignment into one that he/she can complete. In addition, your kid will be exposed to the social and emotional benefits of cooperation, which is critical for his/her long-term development. You must devote more time, but it is a worthwhile investment.

3. Get realistic expectations about the development of empathy and kindness.

Kids continue to learn about emotions throughout their childhood, including how to control their own moods and read other people's minds.

Young kids are more readily threatened because they are dependent, inexperienced, and fragile. As a result, they are more prone to focus on preserving their own interests.

Older kids may also react in this way if they believe the world is unfriendly or unfair.

Furthermore, some kids have a physiological disadvantage. They are capable of learning about social cues, but their brains do not reward them as well. As a result, kids are less likely to learn independently. They require our assistance.

So, while your kid's behavior may appear selfish, it doesn't necessarily imply that he/she is incorrigibly self-absorbed.

From a young age, kids show a propensity for empathy and kindness. Even babies appear to cheer for the underdog.

When kids fail to demonstrate concern for others, it's usually because they don't understand the situation or can't control their impulses. They require opportunities to learn, including building stable relationships with us, communicating about their feelings and those of others, witnessing excellent role models, and growing up in an environment that encourages self-control and collaboration.

4.   **Focus on maintaining a positive relationship.**

Parents fall into a classic trap, according to researchers.

Parents tend to focus on all of the daily issues when their kids misbehave frequently. They feel obligated to respond to every offense with criticism or punishment, resulting in a relationship dominated by negative interactions.

It's a depressing outcome that's also counterproductive. According to research, when we give kids positive feedback for making excellent choices rather than threats and punishments for doing the wrong thing, they are more likely to learn desirable social skills.

Furthermore, a negative diet can make kids more stubborn. Negative parenting can set off a chain reaction of misbehavior, punishment, revenge, more punishment, and misbehavior.

How do you maintain your calm and cheerful demeanor? It's not easy, especially if your kid appears to be trapped in "defiance mode." You'll require social support as well as possible professional assistance. According to studies, therapists who are specifically educated in dealing with kid aggression can assist reduce stress and improve behavior.

The so-called "Oregon Model" of Parent Management Training is one approach.

Parents learn effective ways to set limits, develop cooperation, resolve conflicts in a healthy manner, and infuse daily life with enjoyable, loving activities through weekly coaching and role acting sessions. The first step, though, is to reorganize your priorities. It is more vital to maintain positive relationships than to prosecute every failure. It's sometimes necessary to pick and choose your battles.

5. Don't sacrifice your own psychological well-being

Dealing with violence is a difficult situation, and tension is painful. It makes us sick, causes us to think erratically, and harms our relationships.

Stress is contagious: Our negative sentiments are picked up by even the tiniest of kids.

When parents are worried, it only adds to the fire, their kid's behavior issues tend to worsen.

So, taking care of yourself shouldn't be an afterthought or a luxury to be postponed until your kid's behavior issues improve. It's a critical issue and a key participant in the situation.

2.2 Why Transitions Trigger Problem Behavior

Transitions are a common behavior trigger for many youngsters. Transitions in many families may become a flashpoint that everyone learns to dread, whether it's getting ready for bed, coming to dinner, or putting down the video game controller. If your child struggles with transitions, it's critical to figure out what aspects of the shift are challenging. Kids often dislike having to stop doing something they enjoy (such as playing on the internet) in order to do something less enjoyable (such as getting ready to leave the house).

While no one appreciates having to put a halt to something enjoyable, some children have a harder time with it than others. This could indicate that their emotional self-regulation skills are still developing, although it is only one possible cause. Other kids have a hard time dealing with unexpected schedule adjustments or moving on from something they don't feel they've completed.

Transitional difficulties in children can be an indication of a mental health problem. Transitions are especially difficult for children with ADHD, autism, anxiety, and OCD.

Techniques to make transitions easier

You can start thinking about what you believe might assist once you've narrowed down what you think is causing your child's reluctance to transition. (Note: Taking your concerns to a clinician is critical if you suspect your child has an undiagnosed mental health condition.)

You might wish to try the following techniques

A sneak peeks and a countdown: Create a schedule for the day every morning. Give a timeframe and description of what will happen before each transition, as well as countdowns (in 20 minutes, then 10, then five, it will be time to finish breakfast and head to school). This aids children's emotional preparation.

To get their attention, do the following: Make a special effort to attract the attention of children who have trouble focusing.

Make eye contact with them, sit next to them, place your hand on their shoulder, or ask them to repeat what you've said back to you. It increases their likelihood of following through.

Make use of music: Songs can assist children (particularly young children) in easing into transitions. The "clean up" song is a good example, but there are plenty of other songs that may be found or made up to fit a range of scenarios, from tying shoes to cleaning teeth.

Visual hints: A visual reminder for youngsters is to post a chart with illustrations illustrating what to expect from a particular transition or the processes needed.

Make a routine: Build some regularity and structure into any transitions that your child suffers with on a daily basis, such as going to bed. When it's time to go to bed, for example, your child can choose one last thing he/she wants to do. Then you both head upstairs to clean your teeth and read a story before turning off the lights. Consistently following this schedule helps children understand what to expect and makes the transition easier.

Use prizes: Until children have become accustomed to them, rewards can be an excellent technique for easing difficult transitions. Snacks, stickers, or a point system that leads to concrete rewards can be used by parents.

Consider what repercussions you are (or are not) delivering if a transition isn't going smoothly. Active ignoring or a time-out may be more effective alternatives than yelling.

Use praise: When a youngster completes a transition, be sure to give him/her some enthusiastic labeled praise to acknowledge his/her achievement. "I appreciated how you handed over the iPad immediately and started brushing your teeth," for example. "We've got more time to read now!"

Skills: How to Do a Time Out

The goal of a time out isn't to shame or penalize your child; rather, it's to calm an emotional situation and teach your child how to handle irritation and self-control. Using a time out to explain that certain behavior is inappropriate is also a good idea.

Time outs have been tried by many parents with varying degrees of effectiveness. Time outs must be done consistently and in a specific order to be successful. If you're learning how to utilize time-outs or want to improve your technique, here are some tips to follow.

Allow for forewarning: Kids must be aware of which behaviors are associated with particular outcomes. Work with your child to determine which behaviors (such as hitting or failing to follow your instructions) will result in a time out, so he/she understands what to expect.

Decide on a location ahead of time: A particular chair or a spot on the stairs might also help a child anticipate what to expect. It's best to call it the time-out chair rather than "the naughty chair" or something similar. When time-outs are used to educate children on how to behave rather than to punish them, they are more effective.

Make use of a snappy retort: When a child misbehaves in one of the ways you've covered, make sure the next time out is taken right away and that you explain why: "No striking! Take a time-out." Be exact, succinct, and emotionless. This ensures that the youngster can connect his/her actions to their consequences. Delayed punishments are ineffective because children believe you are merely punishing them.

Keep it short: One minute per year of age is a common time-out calculation. A timer, according to some experts, is recommended so that a youngster can observe the time being measured.

Keep it calm: During a time out, the idea is for children to sit quietly. Some experts advise waiting until your youngster is quiet before starting the timer.

Others believe it is too difficult for young children. Before the time out is up, the child must be perfectly silent for 5 seconds. This teaches children to associate good behavior with the end of a time out and reinforces the message that yelling and screaming during a timeout will not result in a positive outcome.

Pay no attention: Even if they're moaning, weeping, or protesting, kids in time out should be ignored. Don't talk to them or about them. You're giving the message that misbehaving isn't the method to achieve what they want by withdrawing your attention during the time out.

The importance of consistency cannot be overstated: It's easy to put kids in time out whenever they act badly or press your buttons, but doing so on a whim makes it more difficult for youngsters to understand the link between specific misbehaviors and their consequences.

It's also crucial that the time-out happens every time the precise goal behavior occurs. If you don't, you're encouraging the child to believe he/she can get away with it.

There are no rewarding stimuli: The youngster should not have access to television, electrical gadgets, toys, or games while in the time-out chair. If you're away from home, choose a location that is free of distracting stimulation for the child.

If a child refuses to stay in time out, place him/her in a backup time out space that he/she cannot escape (such as a bedroom without any reinforcing stimuli such as television, toys, or games), and explain that he/she must stay there for one minute and be peaceful and quiet before being allowed to leave. After that, he/she should be returned to the time-out chair, and the time limit for his/her stay should be reset. If he/she gets out of the chair again, the cycle starts all over again. Your child should rapidly learn that staying in the chair until the timer goes off is in his/her best interests.

2.3 After the Time Out

When youngsters are given time-outs for disobeying your directions, they should be asked to do whatever task they were assigned before the time out. This teaches children that time-outs aren't meant to be used as a means of escape.

Once the time out is done, you should resume paying attention to them, listening in to whatever they are doing/working on/playing so that you can "catch them doing good" and congratulate them directly for it. For example, if your child finishes his/her time out and then gently plays with the dog, you should compliment him/her ("I love how nicely you're playing with the dog.

You have such lovely, sensitive hands!") This reassures your child that, despite having to go to time out, he/she is still capable of doing wonderful and positive things that make you pleased and love her.

Skills: How to Give Effective Instructions

If you follow these suggestions, your children will be more likely to understand and obey your instructions:

- Be straightforward. Instead of asking questions, make statements. "Please sit down," rather than "Are you ready to get out your homework?"

- Stay in close proximity. Instead of yelling out from across the room, give directions while you are close to your youngster.

- Issue commands that are clear and specific. "Please go ahead and begin your reading assignment," instead of "Go ahead."

- Give directions that are age-appropriate. Speak to your child on a level that he/she can comprehend. Keep things simple and use terms you know your youngster understands if your child is younger. "Please pick up the ball." It's critical to be explicit without being patronizing with older children.

- Give each person one instruction at a time. Avoid delivering a sequence of orders, especially to children with concentration issues. "Please put on your sneakers, fetch your lunch off the kitchen counter, and meet me in the front hall."

- Keep explanations to a minimum. Giving a rationale can help children pay attention to a command, but not if the command is forgotten in the process. "Get your coat on because it's raining, and I don't want you to catch a cold", for example. Instead, say something like, "It's raining outside, and I don't want you to get a cold. Put on your coat".

- Allow time for children to process. Wait a few seconds after you've given the order before repeating it. Instead of learning that they don't need to listen since the instructions will be repeated, children learn to listen to calm instructions provided only once.

Improving the Parent-Child Relationship

The toll that behavioral disorders have on the family dynamic is one of the most painful side effects. When a child has persistent behavioral challenges, parents frequently do not enjoy their time with their child. This can be aggravating as well as guilt-inducing.

Children are also harmed when they are frequently chastised or pick up on their parents' displeasure, which can lead to resentment and lower self-esteem.

- All families dealing with chronic problem behavior should make improving the parent-child relationship a priority. To that aim, make an effort to increase the frequency of positive interactions you have with your child that does not lead to confrontation. Consider the following scenario:

- Instead of negative comments or focusing on what you don't want to see, use behavior management tactics that reinforce what you do want to see (such as delivering clear instructions in a neutral tone of voice or using lots of positive praise).

- Be aware of your own emotions and seek out appropriate ways to deal with stressful events without exacerbating them. If you need a moment to calm down, use your own emotional self-regulation abilities or take a time out.

- Consider how you can strengthen (or develop) meaningful relationships in every relationship you want to cherish. Are there any shared interests you could pursue? You might be able to build new interpersonal routines.

- Every day, set aside some time to be present and nonjudgmental with your child.

How to establish daily quality time

Even a tiny amount of time set aside every day in a consistent manner can become something that children and their parents look forward to.

This should be a time of positive connection, free of rules or commands, to assist everyone in the family in de-stress and enjoy each other's presence. This should be treated like a special occasion, not something that is dependent on a child's good behavior. Here are some helpful hints:

- With younger children, aim for 5 minutes per day; with teenagers, aim for 15 minutes each day.

- Let your child choose an activity he/she enjoys and engage in with her

- Actively listen and let him/her lead the conversation

- Validate his/her choices and interests

- Focus on excellent rewarding behavior while ignoring minor disobedience

- Avoid directing the activity or criticizing

Chapter 3

Helping Kids Deal With Emotions

Some children act out as a result of their inability to control their emotions. This is a typical issue among young children who have not yet learned the ability to deal constructively with strong emotions. As youngsters get older, some of them continue to battle with self-control. Parents and instructors may observe that they are more sensitive than their siblings or peers and that they have outsized emotional reactions.

The best part is that self-regulation is a skill that can be taught just like any other, and parents can play an important role in assisting children in learning how to manage their emotions, even very strong ones. Here are some ways for assisting children in calming down rather than acting out.

3.1 Developing Emotional IQ

Taking the time to identify and label emotions encourages children to become more aware of their feelings. This is significant because recognizing and acknowledging our emotions is the first step toward learning to manage them. Simply expressing an emotion might sometimes help to defuse it. We often try to act as though we aren't experiencing bad feelings until it is too late and we are miserable. Acknowledging a negative emotion reduces its strength and allows you to begin to consider constructive options for dealing with it. Parents can assist youngsters in learning to accomplish this by demonstrating it in their own actions. If you're irritated because you forgot something in the grocery shop, say something like, "I'm so frustrated right now! I forgot to get milk!" you tell your child. You can then model coping and problem-solving strategies after you've acknowledged how you're feeling. "I'm going to take some deep breaths to calm down - that always works for me," you might say. After that, you can say, "Now how can I fix this problem?" and brainstorm solutions.

Children will begin to catch up on the skills you are modeling for them, but they may require more assistance as they learn to manage their emotions. Ask your child to describe how he/she is feeling if you see he/she is becoming upset. Is he/she able to give it a name?

Just make sure that if your child expresses sadness, anxiety, or anger, you don't try to talk him/her out of it right away. Hearing "Oh, it's not that horrible!" might make children feel as if their emotions are incorrect, thereby teaching them not to disclose how they are feeling. Instead, you might acknowledge the emotion "Yes, that does sound irritating" or "You do appear upset".

Heading off big emotions

Another benefit of a youngster learning to deliberately describe his/her emotions is that it helps him/her to begin paying attention to how he/she feels, which means he/she will be more likely to detect an emotion before it becomes overwhelming.

The intense emotions children display during tantrums often catch parents off guard. Even if it appears that way, kids don't go from peaceful to wailing on the floor in a moment. Emotions rise and fall like a wave. Kids can learn to control overwhelming emotions by recognizing and categorizing them early on before the wave grows too large.

Many children benefit by rating the intensity of their emotions on a scale of one to ten, with one being calm and ten being enraged. You may also use this as a model. You might exclaim that you're at a 4 when you're irritated because you neglected to get milk at the grocery shop. This may seem stupid at first, but it teaches children to take a moment to notice how they are feeling. Something like a feelings thermometer could be useful for kids who want visual aids.

Getting Help

When to get help

Most youngsters suffer tantrums or meltdowns from time to time.

It's normal for kids to act out when it's time to go to bed or stop playing a game. When children have frequent tantrums or appear to be unable to regulate their temper on a regular basis, you may be witnessing something more serious than usual problem behavior.

Here are some warning indicators to look for:

- When his/her conduct makes it difficult for him/her to make friends or get along with other children.

- When a particular conduct is producing a lot of friction in the home and causing family life to be disrupted

- When your child's conduct is making him/her feel horrible about him/herself because he/she can't manage his/her anger

- When his/her behavior is generating problems at school with his/her teachers or fellow pupils

- When his/her behavior is dangerous to him/herself or others

Making an appointment with a doctor who specializes in children's mental health can be quite beneficial if you are concerned about your youngster's behavior and are having difficulty handling it on your own. A clinician can conduct a thorough assessment to see if your kid has an undiagnosed mental health disorder that is contributing to him/her behavior problems, as well as suggesting specific methods or therapies that may be beneficial.

Possible causes and diagnoses

A list of mental health illnesses and other problems that may be linked to disruptive conduct is provided below.

Attention-deficit hyperactivity disorder (ADHD)

Youngsters with ADHD have a hard time concentrating on tasks, paying attention, sitting still, and controlling impulsive behavior.

While disruptive conduct is not an ADHD sign, it is frequently the effect of ADHD symptoms. Impulsivity and inattention can make it difficult for children to handle repetitive, dull, or time-consuming chores. As a result, youngsters with ADHD are frequently frustrated, and their impulsivity can manifest itself in the form of throwing a shoe, pushing someone, or yelling, "shut up!"

Negative behavior patterns might develop in some children with ADHD as a result of years of being in conflict with adults.

Oppositional defiant disorder (ODD)

Arguments with authority figures, refusal to follow the rules, blaming others for their mistakes, being abnormally angry and irritable, and other symptoms are common in children with ODD. These symptoms can occur in any child at any moment.

The severity of ODD and the length of time it has been present distinguish it from regular oppositional behavior.

Disruptive mood dysregulation disorder (DMDD)

Children with DMDD have frequent, intense temper outbursts that appear to be out of proportion to the situation. They are persistently irritated in between tantrums. Their disruptive behavior stems from their strong emotions and lack of self-control. After a tantrum, children with DMDD are frequently contrite.

Anxiety

Children that appear enraged and stubborn may be suffering from extreme anxiety. When youngsters are having difficulty dealing with stressful situations, they may lash out. This might happen when kids are under too much strain at home or at school. Your child's "fight or flight" instinct may kick in in an anxiety-inducing circumstance, and he/she may throw a tantrum or decline to do something to escape the source of intense fear.

Trauma

Children who have been traumatized frequently use violent behavior to disguise their distress. They may struggle with poor emotional self-regulation, negative thinking, and be highly vigilant to hazards as a result of their trauma, making them more likely to activate their "fight or flight" reaction to protect themselves.

Problems with learning

Children who act out in school or while doing homework may be suffering from an undiagnosed learning impairment.

They may be irritated and ashamed because they are having difficulty doing activities that appear to be simple for other children, and they are unsure why. Instead of asking for help, they may shred up homework or act out to distract themselves from their genuine problems.

Issues with sensory processing

Some children struggle to process the sensory information they get from their environment. Children who are under or overly sensitive to stimuli are likely to feel uneasy, anxious, distracted, and overwhelmed, which can lead to disruptive conduct.

Autism

Children on the autism spectrum are prone to rigidity, requiring a steady routine in order to feel secure, and sudden alterations can result in a tantrum. Autistic children can often have sensory difficulties, which can make them feel overwhelmed.

Some autistic youngsters may also struggle to express themselves due to a lack of language and communication abilities.

Parent training programs

Parent training programs are designed to help parents gain the skills they'll need to manage their child's bad behavior and enhance their relationship with their child.

These programs are evidence-based, which means they have been rigorously studied and proved to be successful for many families. They are directed by psychologists and social workers.

The following is a list of several types of parent training, as well as what differentiates them and whose families they may benefit.

Parent-Child Interaction Therapy (PCIT)

PCIT sessions are attended by both parents and children, during which a clinician teaches them how to communicate in a positive, productive manner. It is beneficial for children aged 3-7 years old and typically takes 14 -17 weekly sessions.

Parents receive live coaching (through a bug in the ear) from a therapist who watches them as their child executes a series of exercises, and parents practice precise reactions to both desired and undesired conduct.

Parental Management Training (PMT)

Parents are normally seen without their children in PMT, which is for children aged 3-10, though children may be requested to join in some sessions.

The therapist teaches and models skills for dealing more effectively with challenging behaviors, which are then role-played with parents. Parents are expected to practice the skills at home after each session. Families typically attend at least ten sessions.

When children are too old for PCIT, PMT is a viable alternative because it is acceptable for all ages.

It can also be a useful alternative for families with a great parent-child relationship but youngsters who are battling with anxiety, severe impulsivity, or explosive rage.

Defiant Teens

Defiant Teen is a program for parents of teenagers aged 13-18. Only parents are included in the first half of this program, which focuses on teaching more effective methods for engaging with their teenagers, particularly for dealing with noncompliance or defiant conduct. However, because teens are more independent and less impacted by their parents' supervision than younger children, the program also involves instruction for the adolescent to enable him/her to become a partner in improving the family dynamic.

In the second part, both parents and teenagers receive problem-solving communication training. The goal is to provide family behavioral resources to help each family member improve their problem-solving, negotiating, and communication skills, as well as to rectify any irrational views that may be obstructing their relationships.

Program for Positive Parenting (Triple P)

The Triple P program focuses on providing parents with information and tools to help them gain confidence and self-sufficiency in dealing with their children's conduct. From toddlerhood to puberty, it can be used with a wide spectrum of youngsters. Families can participate in several levels of intervention with Triple P, depending on their needs. In some sessions, clinicians will meet with parents one-on-one to discuss skills and methods, while in others, children will be included, with the therapist providing live coaching.

The Incredible Years

The Incredible Years provides small-group instruction for parents of children ranging in age from infancy to adolescence.

The programs range in length from 12-20 weeks and are divided into four age categories (baby, toddler, preschool, and school-age). Before going on to consistent routines, regulations, and limit-setting, the approach focuses on developing parent-child interactions and positive attachment.

Finally, it discusses child-management techniques like ignoring, redirection, rational and natural consequences, time to relax, and problem-solving.

Incredible Years offers children's classes for children aged four to eight years old that focus on helping them develop emotion control tools and social skills. According to research, the kids' group is effective at improving pro-social conduct and reducing negative behaviors. Parents discover that they can learn from other parents in the group as well as from therapists.

3.2 Medication

Parent training and behavior therapy are thought to be a more effective and long-lasting method of helping children learn to control their unpleasant emotions and disruptive conduct. Medications, on the other hand, are occasionally used in conjunction with behavioral therapy. Antipsychotic drugs, such as Abilify (aripiprazole) and Risperdal (risperidone), have been demonstrated to lessen aggression and irritability in children who are in danger of being removed from school or home, but you can consult your physician before taking these medicines.

If a youngster, especially those with ADHD, shows excessive impulsivity, stimulant medication may be administered. If a youngster has underlying sadness or anxiety, antidepressants (SSRIs) may be beneficial.

It's critical to discuss any concerns you have about your child's treatment plan, progress, or any side effects you're seeing with your doctor. A qualified physician will be prepared to talk about your symptoms and explain your alternatives for adjusting your dosage or medication. You should seek a second opinion if you don't believe your child's doctor is taking your concerns seriously or if your doctor is not following best practices when modifying dosages or introducing new medications. If you believe your child should stop taking medicine, notify your doctor and explore the benefits and drawbacks.

Make no changes or stop taking the drug without first consulting your doctor. Many medications should be tapered off gradually, and children should be watched for withdrawal symptoms.

Note about Risperdal

Risperdal can cause major side effects, such as significant weight gain and potentially dangerous metabolic, neurological, and hormonal alterations. During treatment with Risperdal or any atypical antipsychotic, children should be examined by their doctors on a frequent basis. Before starting treatment, patients should be evaluated for height, weight, vital signs, prolactin, blood fats, and sugar levels to create baselines. A child's levels should be checked periodically throughout the first few months of treatment. If the youngster is taking the drug for a long time, he should be checked once a year.

Behavior Issues in School

Establishing some school-specific behavior management tactics is vital for youngsters who struggle with their behavior in the classroom.

Frequently, the initial step is to request a functional behavior assessment from the school. An FBA's purpose is to learn more about when and why your child is behaving out in class. This information is then utilized to build a strategy for assisting. The FBA is usually led by a school psychologist or behavioral expert, who may speak with you, your child's teachers, and your kid as part of the assessment, as well as observe your child in class.

It's critical to figure out which precise issues your youngster faces. It helps to gather as much information as possible about the real-life conditions that appear to contribute to disruptive conduct, paying attention to what happens immediately before, during, and after the behavior, just as it does at home.

Observing your child when he/she is not acting out can also be instructive. After gathering and analyzing this data, the school psychologist or behavioral specialist can work on developing a behavior intervention plan (BIP) that includes recommendations for preventing problem behaviors and reinforcing positive behavior. Various instructional tactics, different punishments for disobedience, and alterations to regular routines are examples of this. It's crucial to check in on these methods on a regular basis to see how effective they are (and make changes if needed).

How can parents help their youngsters achieve their school behavior goals at home?

Parents can also play a role in reinforcing good school conduct. You may tell your child's teacher that you want to work with them to improve their conduct and choose one or two goals to work on at a time, such as handing in homework and not yelling in class. Then you can request that the instructor provide you with progress updates on your child on a regular basis.

You don't want to annoy the teacher, but if you get a progress report every few days or every week, you can help reinforce the school's goals at home by rewarding good school conduct or enacting appropriate consequences.

For instance, if you hear that your child is doing an excellent job handing in his/her schoolwork, you may reward him/her with some extra screen time over the weekend. You may give him/her a greater reward, such as a trip to his/her favorite restaurant, if he's doing an especially fantastic job.

On the other hand if you get a report that he/she isn't doing his/her assignments, you might tell him/her that he/she won't be getting any screen time for the first two days of the week since he/she needs to focus on his/her homework.

3.3 Do Babies Feel Empathy?

Is it true that babies can tell when you're sad? Do they seem worried? Do newborns have feelings of empathy? Yes!

You may have heard that empathy doesn't fully develop until preschool. However, that is a grave misrepresentation of the evidence. Affective empathy and cognitive empathy are two types of empathy recognized by scientists, and research clearly shows that babies experience both.

Take, for example, affective empathy. This is also known as "emotional contagion," and it occurs when your emotions cause me to experience comparable feelings.

Within the first few days following birth, babies show signs of emotional contagion.

When they hear other newborns cry, they grow distressed. Researchers have conducted tests in which babies were exposed to control stimuli, such as computer-synthesized crying, to show that it isn't just a response to noise.

When babies hear the screams of a real baby, they weep even harder. Babies are fascinated by faces and begin to learn about facial emotions at a young age. By six weeks after birth, babies begin to return our smiles, and they feel distressed if we stare at them with unresponsive facial expressions. Babies may be able to recognize some of their mothers' emotional facial expressions, three and a half months after birth. Babies, for example, appeared to expect their moms to sound joyful when they looked happy and sad when they looked sad in one experiment.

Young newborns, like adults, replicate the joy they observe in another person's face.

Babies have a unique type of physiological, emotional contagion between the ages of four and six months, which may be seen in their eyes.

When we're aroused, our pupils dilate, which is a potent social cue that causes a mirroring reaction, looking into the eyes of someone with dilated pupils causes your pupils to expand. Experiments demonstrate that babies react similarly to adults.

Babies show symptoms of sympathetic care for those in distress towards the end of their first year.

When their moms appear worried, kids display concern by the age of ten months. They may also express much more sympathetic care for their upset peers.

So, according to a number of studies involving newborns who were tested in a variety of ways, neonates experience affective empathy before they can speak. Another piece of evidence has also convinced me. Nonhuman animals, especially baby rats, have been shown to have affective empathy.

It appears absurd to believe that human infants are incapable of performing tasks that a mouse, for example, can perform.

Don't be fooled by uneducated writers and self-proclaimed "baby experts" who claim that babies can't perceive or replicate other people's emotions.

Another type of empathy I described as cognitive empathy. What do you think about that?

Affective empathy can be triggered automatically, as I mentioned earlier. You don't have to think about the repercussions if you see someone who is afraid.

Simply put, you're becoming more worried and agitated.

Cognitive empathy is not the same as emotional empathy. It's what you do when you're trying to find out why someone is afraid, and it necessitates a shift in perspective as well as purposeful, focused thought. It's more of a mental exercise in the vein of Sherlock Holmes. And your ability to succeed is mostly determined by your knowledge, experience, and emotional self-control.

If a terrified man clutches his chest and writhes in pain, you could assume he's having a heart attack or is reacting to a sudden injury. But what if you had no medical training and had never seen anybody act this way before?

Affective empathy may be triggered by the exhibition of emotion. Your ability to express cognitive empathy, on the other hand, would be severely constrained.

You'd have a hard time comprehending the scenario, and you'd have no idea what kind of assistance to offer.

As a result, background information is critical for demonstrating cognitive empathy, and babies have clear disadvantages. They have only a limited understanding of the world.

They aren't aware of all the things that can cause others to become emotional. How about emotional self-discipline? Although the link between empathy and affective empathy is less obvious, it is critical, especially if you have a lot of affective empathy. What is the reason for this? Emotional contagion can cause you to concentrate on your own feelings rather than the feelings of others.

Let's return to the worried man who is experiencing a heart attack. Being in his presence is unsettling. You might be able to "catch" his anxiety and distress. You must maintain your focus on the man's needs in order to respond with cognitive empathy — and sympathetic concern. His emotions are not yours. However, if the situation is causing you anxiety, this may be difficult. You may feel compelled to turn away. It can also happen when you're feeling happy. Someone else's joyful anticipation may be too much for you. That's why you'll occasionally notice a newborn tilt his/her head away from social encounters. He/she is closing his/her eyes. The scenario is far too energizing. The baby is overstimulated and is attempting to unplug from the source of stimulus. As a result, developing cognitive empathy necessitates some emotional self-control. You must really be able to emotionally remove yourself from whatever is going on. Not to the point that you are no longer affected by emotional contagion.

But only enough so that you can consider the other person's viewpoint and wants clearly.

Is there any evidence of cognitive empathy in babies? Yes!

Many of the components of cognitive empathy appear to be present in experiments. Babies who are six months old, for example, appear to be aware of victimization and have a preference for approaching others who have been abused.

However, the important point here is that babies are aware of the emotional effects of social interactions. They appear to recognize that when people are bullied, they are distressed.

When offered the option of approaching a well-treated person or a victim of bullying, babies are more likely to approach the victim. There have also been instances where older babies have offered instrumental assistance.

According to other research, some babies will try to aid other babies.

In one experiment, researchers swaddled a realistic-looking baby doll, obscuring the majority of the doll's face so that spectators wouldn't realize it wasn't a real baby. The doll was then fitted with an audio device by the researchers. It replayed recordings of a sobbing infant. The babies, aged 12-24 months, were left alone with the sobbing doll by the researchers.

What occurred after that? The majority of the babies had worried expressions on their faces, and some approached the swaddled figure in an attempt to comfort it. They attempted to provide a toy for the "baby."

This behavior manifested itself without any provocation or bribery. When babies saw what they thought was a distraught baby, they reacted in ways that implied cognitive empathy. They were undoubtedly aware from previous experience that a toy can lift an infant's spirits. They look to have done some perspective-taking and come up with a suitable solution.

What about mental theory?

You may have heard that babies lack theory of mind or the ability to attribute mental states to others. And this appears to be a challenge for cognitive empathy.

It's difficult to determine what someone needs if you have no knowledge of his/her views, desires, or opinions!

However, when it comes to the theory of mind, babies aren't completely clueless.

Most babies can deduce another person's intentions before the age of five months, such as grabbing an object. As a result, babies may be better prepared to comprehend the emotional ramifications of having one's ambitions denied.

While the exact time is debatable, research suggests that by the age of two, many kids will have begun to demonstrate more sophisticated abilities. They may understand, for example, that other people can believe incorrect information. Alternatively, they may discover that not everyone likes the same meals. Even if they loathe broccoli, they understand why you might want to eat it.

There's a lot more to learn about other people's thinking, and babies don't have the same level of understanding as adults. However, babies understand some things – enough to empathize in a range of situations.

So, where does empathy originate? What causes babies to feel empathy?

As we've already mentioned, cognitive empathy is influenced by your past experiences and knowledge. It also depends on your motivation. Are you able to empathize with another person's situation? Do you wish to lend a hand? Do you believe this person deserves your assistance? Cognitive empathy isn't something that just happens. It takes time to develop a willingness to assist others. It is, to a considerable extent, learned.

Biological researchers believe that the same is true for affective empathy, and I agree with them.

They claim that babies pick up on affective empathy through association. When a baby is happy, and his/her mother responds by smiling and making pleasant sounds, the infant learns to correlate his/her own happiness with the mother's social signals. After that, the brain will associate grins and giggles with positive inner emotion. Similarly, babies can quickly learn to "wire together" different emotions and social cues. When a baby experiences fear while also observing signals of fear in another person, the brain creates a relationship between the two. When a baby is upset and hears someone weeping, he/she learns to identify unhappiness with sobbing.

It's a plausible theory and one that should make us think twice. A caregiver's role in the development of emotional empathy is critical. We can help a newborn develop empathy by paying attention to his/her moods and mimicking those emotions with compassionate facial expressions, sounds, and gestures.

As a result, empathy is not a natural trait. We can't assume that each new generation will develop empathy, regardless of the social milieu or child-rearing practices to which they are exposed.

Parents are important. Peers are important. Ideologies and social norms are important. We must be emotionally responsive to our infants in order to foster empathy. We must provide an example of sensitivity and kindness when dealing with others. We must teach them to broaden rather than narrow their circle of people with whom they may empathize. We must teach children how to be mindful and reflective. Being knowingly and purposely kind.

Yes, babies are empathetic. Yes, they are born with the intention of showing compassion and kindness to those who are in need.

Chapter 4

Emotion Coaching and Tips for Parents

4.1 Tips for Being a Better Emotion Coach

Does your child's behavior make you anxious? Take care of yourself so you can address the situation calmly, with realistic expectations and empathy.

It's crucial not to take your child's misbehavior too seriously. Here we have a full talk about managing angry or defiant children, as well as some parental stress management tips.

Angry tantrums, striking, kicking, or biting; hot-headed outbursts that destroy property; cool-headed bullying; verbal attacks; attempts to dominate others by threats or violence are all examples of kid aggression.

(4.1.1) Twelve evidence-based Tips for making Life Better

Parenting stress affects the entire family, robbing everyone of patience, destroying relationships, and eroding well-being. What are our options?

Here are some ideas based on the most recent research.

1. Do you require social assistance? Even if it's simply a phone call to a parenting helpline, reach out.

It should come as no surprise, but having friends, family, or neighbors on your side makes parenting a whole lot simpler.

Human parents have always needed assistance. People who provide childcare, emotional support, and financial assistance.

So, if you're feeling lonely and overwhelmed, realize that it's not a sign of weakness. Isolation isn't something you're intended to do. You're not supposed to be stressed out. You're expected to be a part of a social network that supports you.

But what if you don't live near your friends and family? Or do you lack the individuals in your life who can offer you the support you require?

There are numerous possibilities: Parenting cooperatives in the area. Parenting networks and support groups can be found online. Therapists who have undergone extensive training.

Enrolling in a parenting course might also be beneficial. Parenting lessons, according to studies, can help you feel less angry, guilty, and stressed, especially if your child has challenging behavior issues.

2. Limit your contact with negative thoughts and media.

It's human nature to seek out patterns. You might be convinced that if a youngster is temperamental, disobedient, or high-strung, his/her next action will be bad. When you're agitated, furious, or worried, it's normal to pay extra attention to potential hazards.

Stress causes people to focus on the negative aspects of their lives. However, your biases and preconceptions might become self-fulfilling. You're more likely to inspire unpleasant conduct from others if you presume the worst. You're also more likely to fall into a downward spiral of a bad mood.

People tend to give more attention to distressing visuals, threatening statements, and negative feedback after a brief exposure to negative emotional content. They relive painful experiences or are concerned about the future.

Such ideas trigger the brain's stress pathways, generating even more worry and depression. A single trigger — an enraged remark, an unpleasant remembrance, or a painful narrative — could be all it takes to start the process.

This could be beneficial in certain crisis situations.

When a lion is stalking you, it's a good idea to go to threat mode. In some circumstances, however, you're in a far worse situation. Overdosing on frightening material and negative news does more than only increase your stress levels in the short term. It also makes it difficult for you to think critically and solve difficulties. And everyone suffers as a result: you, your family, your neighbors, and your employees.

There is a simple approach for self-defense: Avoid unnecessarily exposing yourself to negative feelings.

- Turn off distracting media;
- avoid aggressive, impolite, or judgmental people;
- consider taking a different route to work if avoiding noise, pollution, difficulties, hostility, and other stressors is a priority.

3. Focus on the positive: acts of kindness, warmth, and compassion.

We've already seen how negative messages can cause your stress reaction to spiral out of control. The opposite is also true, by downloading positive content to our brains, we can promote happy moods.

So look for enjoyable social interactions, notice your child's smiles, and take advantage of opportunities to provide physical affection. Reminisce about joyful times, read inspirational stories, crack jokes, and pet the family dog.

All of these factors have been found to shift brain chemistry away from stress and toward serenity and well-being.

The stress reaction can be deactivated by focusing on acts of compassion and social support, even if they are committed by strangers in a photograph. When we think about other people's compassionate and helpful behavior, we feel less intimidated.

4. Make use of psychological knowledge to assist your future self.

P.G. Wodehouse's comedy books are a good example of this. Jeeves, the manservant of G. Wodehouse, always knows what others will require – even before they do. By utilizing modern psychology concepts, you can take steps to become your own Jeeves.

How do you think you'll react in the future? Experiments show that people have a hard time anticipating future discomforts.

We have a hard time anticipating how hungry we'll become later when we're full, so we don't plan accordingly. We underestimate how bad we'll feel if we don't get enough sleep while we're rested. We think we're good at forecasting these things, but when researchers compare our predictions to actual results, it's evident that we're underestimating our future requirements. So think about what's going wrong and make a conscious effort to aid your future self. Is that game going to cause a brawl among the kids?

If that's the case, don't bring it with you. Is that thorny relative going to be a source of worry for you?

Make a decision about what you'll do about it ahead of time. Will the noise drive you insane? Bring earplugs with you.

5. Allow for more time to complete tasks.

Time pressure is a common source of stress, although it affects some parents more than others.

Mothers are more impacted by time pressure than fathers, according to Scandinavian researchers, and the women who are most affected are either highly educated, financially pressured, or lack social support.

You may believe that you cannot afford to rearrange your schedule, but consider the following: Time pressure may be harmful, and one of the more well-replicated results in psychology is that people frequently underestimate how long it takes to complete tasks.

Furthermore, when compared to adults, young children take longer to react, check their urges, and learn. Little children move at a snail's pace.

As a result, many families are likely to benefit from lowered expectations. If being late drives you mad, get up earlier, and don't assume your slow-poke is attempting to stop you.

6. Re-evaluate the scenario when unpleasant things happen.

It really doesn't matter how many positive thoughts you have, stressful events occur. Yet there are a number of things you may do to deal with the unexpected events that crop up.

People handle stress better when they analyze the matter from a different perspective, according to studies.

Patients with HIV, for example, have a higher quality of life when they concentrate on the positive aspects of their lives, such as improved personal relationships. And it appears that even a small amount of positive thinking can have a significant impact on how we feel.

7. Is your ability to empathize causing you anxiety? Get in touch with your empathic nature's more rational, problem-solving side.

When your child is unhappy, you feel him/her anguish, which can be a wonderful thing since it motivates you to help. But the problem with this type of empathy, which psychologists refer to as "affective empathy," is that it has two sides.

"Feeling the agony" can motivate you to be empathetic, but it can also push you to the limit.

That's perhaps why, when their children are distressed, parents who consider themselves highly empathic can overreact. They become overly anxious, which might cause them to become irritable, harsh, or dominating.

8. Find practical sleep solutions, but don't be concerned about lost hours or exhaustion.

Sleep deprivation makes life tough, so you want to address sleep issues as soon as possible. However, some disturbances are unavoidable, particularly when you have young children. So, what are your options? It should be obvious what not to do at this point. It won't help if you become resentful, ruminate, or fret about your incapacity to operate the next day. Negative thoughts activate your brain's stress circuits, as we've seen, so worrying will make it even more difficult to fall asleep when you finally get the chance.

Furthermore, your children are likely to perceive your emotions, which will make it more difficult for them to sleep.

9. Assist children in coping with their own stressors, and teach siblings how to resolve conflicts.

Emotional self-regulation is not something that children are born with. They need to develop it, and they look to us for guidance. According to research, parents can have a significant impact on how their children deal with stress, especially if they have "difficult" or high-strung temperaments.

It begins with the decisions we make as infants and continues throughout childhood: Preschoolers can benefit from calm, happy, constructive discussions about emotions as they develop strong social skills, empathy, and self-control.

It's also important for toddlers to learn how to get along with their siblings, and it pays to be proactive.

10. Make time for creativity.

Some things lead to happiness because they provide us with immediate, selfish pleasure; others provide us with a more enduring, meaningful pleasure.

When it comes to stress reduction, are they all the same? According to research, this is not the case.

Toxic stress appears to prevent meaningful happiness by changing our DNA and raising our risk of stress-related disease. On the other hand self-gratifying bliss does not. So, if your hectic schedule has caused you to neglect your own satisfaction, consider the following:

Your feeling of significance or purpose isn't a selfish indulgence to be sacrificed for the sake of family obligation. Experiences that generate lasting satisfaction are an important tool for staying fit and protecting your family from second-hand stress. Find ways to reconnect with the experiences, people, and goals that truly matter to you to bring more meaningful happiness into your life.

11. Take advantage of nature's stress-relieving properties.

Spending time outside in a natural setting can help to relieve stress, anger, bewilderment, and despair. Cortisol levels can also be reduced.

12. Get out and get some exercise, but make it enjoyable.

Aerobic exercise helps to protect the body from the negative consequences of physical and mental stress.

It may also lift your mood, reduce anxiety, and stimulate the development of new neurons in your brain. However, experiments show that these outcomes are dependent on the freedom to choose. Exercise that is forced - involuntary — has been shown to increase stress levels.

(4.1.2) Twelve evidence-based suggestions for dealing with Anger, Resistance, and Acting out in Disruptive Behavior Problems

Acts of disruption, aggressiveness, disobedience or anti-social intent are referred to as "externalizing" actions by psychologists. Almost every parent has to deal with them at some point, especially when their children are toddlers. Young children are still learning how to control their emotions and impulses; therefore, they must be taught what is expected of them.

According to studies, more than two-thirds of American preschoolers have temper tantrums.

However, even during early infancy, certain children appear to be more prone to externalizing behavior. What should we do about these issues with behavior?

There isn't a single solution. Children are individuals. What is effective for one child may not be effective for another.

However, research reveals that there are a few general concepts that can be used to enhance collaboration while keeping aggression in check. Here are some suggestions based on research.

1. Look at the big picture: In order to stay connected and improve, children require strong relationships.

Keeping the peace in some families is a relatively simple task.

The children are frequently agreeable, making it easier for caregivers to have a positive attitude and be actively involved. Kids feel more safe, attached, and responsive to learning strong social skills when they have a continuous diet of pleasant family interactions.

It's even more difficult when children are unruly, disrespectful, or aggressive. To stay connected, these children want positive reinforcement. Their misbehavior, on the other hand, irritates anger, frustrates, and depresses us.

Defiant children are, in some ways, their own worst enemies since they are stuck with behavior patterns that drive people to react negatively.

Parents are frequently driven into unproductive behaviors, such as being excessively harsh in certain circumstances or being too disengaged in others.

What is the solution?

Clinical psychologists advise harried parents to pick their battles. You can't expect to police every part of your child's behavior if he/she has externalizing behavior problems. Instead, consider a "quota system" for each discipline.

Ensure that violent, anti-social behavior – behaviors that inflict harm, damaged feelings, or bodily injury — is strictly prohibited. This behavior must be clearly communicated to children. According to studies, children who engage in any form of aggressiveness, even non-physical aggression, are likely to escalate if not addressed.

Other sorts of misconduct should be addressed next, but only if you can do so without tipping the scales. You want to make sure that the majority of your communication appears supportive rather than dismissive, punitive, or prohibitive.

You'll be more likely to maintain a good influence and direct your child's growth over time if you focus on the general emotional tone of the relationship rather than the minutiae of the most recent, minor transgression.

2. Assist children in the development of socio-emotional skills and lead them away from circumstances that are beyond their current capabilities.

It takes a long time for children to gain a sophisticated grasp of emotions. They're a work in progress; they're still gathering information about how humans think and act, and they're also attempting to figure out their own emotions.

And they have a distinct disadvantage when it comes to patience, following directions, reconciling competing demands, remembering plans, and controlling their impulses: their brains are still developing these talents. What happens if we forget this — or if we overestimate a child's developmental limitations inadvertently? Imposing age-inappropriate expectations, such as expecting a 3-year-old to sit quietly over a long restaurant lunch, isn't just a prescription for disaster.

If children are subjected to such unrealistic expectations on a frequent basis, they may fall behind in their overall development. Children require a generally pleasant environment in order to be engaged, motivated, and attentive. They must experience the social advantages of following directions and controlling their emotions in order to learn good citizenship.

They miss out on these possibilities when we put kids in settings that are beyond their capacities, and they acquire the incorrect lessons: that they can't reach our standards; that we're harsh or arbitrary; and that our demand on cooperation means "I win, you lose."

As a result, it's critical to pay attention to your child's existing skill set and avoid situations that are too demanding. Giving kids things they can accomplish — jobs that are either within their developmental zone or just a little tough — teaches them about social achievement and allows them to flourish.

These developmentally sensitive strategies are recommended by researchers and therapists:

- Clearly and calmly state your expectations, emphasizing positive options rather than prohibitions.

  Don't be overbearing with your children; research shows that this type of micromanagement hinders the development of self-control. However, if children stray from the path, give them pleasant reminders of what they should be doing. They may be unable to maintain concentration due to a lack of working memory capacity and attention abilities.

- Have a discussion with your children about how emotions work. What causes people to become enraged or depressed? How can we calm down these emotions or prevent them from arising in the first place? Children who are exposed to these issues as a youngster have better results, and classroom interventions aimed at improving children's socio-emotional awareness result in improved behavior.

Don't try to force a rapid, adult pace on children who are unable to keep up. Children's reaction rates are slower, and they take longer to move from one task to the next. Allow additional time for kids to put their plans into action, and give them a few minutes' notice before switching activities.

- Recognize and remove hot button triggers. Instead of pressing your preschooler to share his/her favorite toy with a visiting friend, ask him/her to put it away before the visit. Allow the children to play with something less emotionally "charged."

- When youngsters get things right, give them supportive, positive feedback. It's a tremendous tool for changing people's minds. However, be aware of which sorts of praise succeed and which types backfire.

- Eliminate unneeded temptations and distractions. When you have a video game console in your sights, it's difficult to focus on your studies.

3. Recognize why children retaliate.

What appears to be defiance in very young toddlers is generally something else. A failure to control impulses, manage emotions, remember rules, or predict how other people will feel. Similar issues may arise in older children.

Some children, for example, may struggle with short-term memory, making it difficult for them to follow orders.

Defiance, on the other hand, is based on children's views about autonomy and fairness in many properly growing children. Kids understand that we have the right to demand certain things, such as rules against violence. However, they believe there are boundaries, and they are more likely to regard our authority as illegitimate if we go beyond those limits.

4. Play developmentally appropriate games that reinforce self-control and prosocial behavior.

You might not feel like having fun and games when you're dealing with a disobedient or violent child. Youngsters, on the other hand, learn via play, and studies show that specific types of play can assist children in learning to interact with others.

For example, a recent experimental study found that after being randomly assigned to play self-regulation games like "Simon Says" (which requires careful listening and self-restraint) and "Musical Statues" (which requires kids to move — and freeze — on cue), young children (aged 3-4 years) experienced improvements in aggressive behavior problems.

More broadly, there is evidence that a variety of enjoyable social activities can aid in the development of social awareness and collaboration abilities in children.

5. Don't overlook the importance of sleep.

It's no secret that sleep has an impact on our mood, but lack of sleep does more than just make us grumpy. It makes it difficult to understand facial expressions, resulting in miscommunication and conflict. In addition, research shows that sleep problems are linked to externalizing behavior.

Adolescents who were subjected to a sleep restriction schedule displayed more "oppositional behavior," such as rage, bickering, and spitefulness, in one study.

Another study found that young infants with early tendencies to oppose authority were particularly vulnerable to the consequences of sleep deprivation. They were more likely to develop externalizing behavior problems over time than other poor sleepers.

In children with autism spectrum disorder, sleep is also linked to disruptive behavior issues. Researchers discovered that children with sleep issues were more aggressive, irritated, and distracted in a recent study.

There's also evidence that lack of sleep causes hyperactivity and focus problems. Preschoolers with sleep issues, for example, are more likely to acquire these symptoms, and children with ADHD might suffer significant deterioration if they don't get enough sleep. In one study, a group of ADHD kids was put on a sleep schedule that cut their nightly sleep time by one hour. After six days, the children's attention abilities had deteriorated to the point that they were clinically significant.

Furthermore, it indicates that treating a child's sleep issues can alleviate symptoms of attention deficit and hyperactivity.

Researchers showed that enhancing sleep in ADHD patients resulted in better classroom behavior and fewer externalizing behavior problems in a randomized, controlled trial. Improved sleep may be able to completely eliminate symptoms in some children.

6. Take care of yourself.

When your child is throwing a tantrum, it's difficult to remain calm and collected, and your own tension makes everything worse - even your child's behavior.

According to studies, when parents alter their own expectations, seek help, and reduce their own stress levels, their children's performance improves.

7. Create an environment that promotes healthy sibling relationships.

We all know how harmful parental abuse and peer aggression are to children. Aggressors get more aggressive over time. Victims are at a heightened danger of experiencing mental illnesses such as anxiety or depression.

Victimization can also lead to externalizing behavioral problems in some people. Bullied children grow up to be bullies. But what about sibling rivalry? Is it a benign experience if your brother strikes or abuses you? Is it part of the natural process of growing up?

The response to this question in modern studies is a resounding "no." When studies look at the effects of sibling hostility on children's outcomes, they find that it has the same bad consequences as other forms of aggressiveness.

Even after researchers adjusted for shared genetics, antisocial behavior amongst siblings fuels the fires of externalizing behavior.

When children argue, the quality of parenting declines. Stressed parents are more likely to employ harsh tactics, make arbitrary and unfair decisions, and withdraw from their children's lives.

As a result, the practice of kindness and collaboration should begin at home. When we teach and enforce fair play rules, our siblings' relationships improve.

We can establish an environment that encourages the development of self-control by showing siblings how to negotiate their own compromises and intervening when such negotiations fail. We can reduce jealousy by teaching older children about their younger siblings' developmental limitations and rewarding them for acting with kindness and responsibility.

8. Teach children to question their preconceived notions.

Even when it isn't true, some people read hatred into the motives of others. This causes them to act irrationally, resulting in a self-fulfilling prophecy. They agitate people who would have otherwise seen them as neutral or nice.

As a result, it's critical to assist children in becoming more adaptable, easygoing, and optimistic. When we offer forth alternative causes for seemingly negative conduct in young children, they benefit.

He/she isn't enraged with you; he/she is simply having a lousy day.

He/she wasn't trying to injure you; it was just a game.

When researchers asked young children (ages 4 - 9) to ponder such possibilities, the children's attitudes shifted.

When it came to hostile attributions, children were less likely to have a bias.

Older children may also benefit, especially if we teach them about the malleability of personality. Kids aren't born with the sense or ability to be "good" or "evil." Kids are sensitive to their surroundings, adaptable, and impacted by their surroundings.

Adolescents didn't merely become more forgiving of human conduct when researchers taught them about flexibility. They were also less prone to see hostility in ordinary, ambiguous gestures.

When children imagined a hypothetical situation, such as someone bumping into them in a crowded hallway, they were more likely to believe it was unintentional. They were also half as likely to indicate they would retaliate aggressively.

A similar study discovered that children who had been taught about personality malleability reacted differently to mock bullying scenarios. They described themselves as less prone to seek revenge than students in a control group.

9. Teach children how to manage their bad emotions by recalling the people who have been supportive in their lives.

You've probably heard that instructing an angry child to take a deep breath and count to ten is a good idea.

That is excellent advice. However, research reveals that we can educate children to utilize the power of thought — and love — to defuse their unpleasant feelings.

Something happened in the brains of volunteers who were reminded of trustworthy social interactions by being shown "feel good" images of individuals being nice and supportive. The threat-response system was momentarily disabled, causing them to be less susceptible to angry expressions.

10. Teach children to recognize moral disengagement mechanisms.

Anti-social behavior is sometimes seen to be a symptom of a lack of empathy. However, many acts of aggression are performed by persons who have strong empathy and social skills.

11. Use disciplinary methods that encourage problem-solving.

According to studies, excessive punishment might cause children to develop increasingly worse behavior issues.

Certain sorts of criticism might make children believe they are innately terrible or inferior, rendering them unable to change. Children that are spanked frequently (more than once a month), tend to become more aggressive over time. Shame methods, on the other hand, might foster resentment and wrath rather than remorse.

So, what should a parent do? It's a bad idea to ignore hostility. Research indicates that parents who engage in aggressive conduct or allow their children to have tantrums are more likely to see their children's behavior deteriorate over time.

However, there is another option: We may concentrate on teaching kids concrete lessons about impulse control, problem-solving, conflict resolution, and making amends.

When researchers tested different disciplinary approaches, they found that spanking, scolding, and telling a child to sit in a corner were not the most effective. The most effective strategies combined non-physical sanctions with explanation, such as explaining the laws and their purpose and talking with kids about how to avoid getting into trouble.

There's also evidence to believe that teaching youngsters real social skills like how to reach an agreement or repair the damage after a fight can help them avoid aggression and win peer acceptance.

Experiments reveal that when their transgressors apologize and try to put things right, 6 and 7 year olds are far more forgiving. If you've accidentally knocked over another child's block tower, helping to repair it could make a great difference.

12. Seek expert help if you're worried about something or if your youngster is having difficulties.

If your child is exceptionally stubborn, reasoning with him/her may feel like a pipe dream. If he/she has attention problems or emotional issues, it may seem impossible. If you're stumped by your youngster — or if something bothers you — seek expert help.

Red flags are behaviors that indicate your child is at risk for an emotional or behavioral disorder.

For example, if your toddler has developed a history of unusually frequent, long, or intense temper tantrums — or appears to lose his/her temper "out of the blue" — you should contact your pediatrician. Researchers also advise parents to seek medical help if they notice their children participating in risky conduct. However, this does not suggest that you must wait for these precise signals to seek assistance.

Children may exhibit disruptive conduct for a variety of reasons. Some children may have difficulty reading the motives and feelings of others. Some children may have difficulty comprehending their own feelings. Some children may experience learning or language disabilities.

Hyperactivity, impulsivity, attention deficiencies, working memory problems, too much stress, and therefore less sleep can all affect children. A child behavior specialist can likely help you better understand what's going on — and identify strategies to improve the situation — whatever your child's specific challenges are. Solicit information about local diagnostic and counseling services from your pediatrician or local school, and don't give up if these services fall short of your expectations. It's possible that you'll have to test a few different approaches before you find the one that works best for you.

(4.1.3) Ten Substitutes for Spanking

Spanking is only a short-term fix for persistent issues. After receiving a spanking, a child frequently asks themselves, "What should I do differently so I don't get slapped again?" Instructions on what the child has to do or stop doing are rarely given after spankings.

Typically, it is nothing more than the parent venting their anger at the youngster. Instead of instilling in a youngster a sense of good and evil, it teaches them to obey out of fear.

It teaches kids that using violence to resolve conflicts is OK. Children who are frequently spanked are more likely to exhibit aggressive behavior, low self-esteem, lying, cheating, sadness, and bullying.

The act of spanking is a great example of how it is okay to hit someone when you are angry or upset.

Ten substitutes for spanking that you may find useful are listed below.

1. Offer options. On the terms of the parents, a choice offers the youngster some control back. Children of really good decision-makers are more obedient and capable of making good choices.

2. Take a break. You, as the parent, do so. It is acceptable to say we will discuss this later; I'm too upset to deal with you right now.

3. Get another person interested. Ask someone who is not as closely connected to the matter to assist you if you feel that your child has made you so upset that you may not be in control. By doing this, you are less likely to hit your kid.

4. Inform them of your expectations. Teach them what they can do differently rather than punish them for acting inappropriately. "Please hang your coat up in the closet next time. How can we make sure you do this"?

5. Recognize the good things they do. Tell them how much you appreciate it when they hang up that coat. Too frequently, parents only focus on their kids' bad actions and ignore the good things they do.

6. Timeout. For every year of their age, the normal rule is one minute. The fact that you are linking the misbehavior to the consequence is more crucial than the environment in which the timeout occurs. Try to create a calm environment where the youngster can't distract you or receive an unintended reward.

When a youngster has calmed down and can control their temper tantrum for the duration of the timeout, the timeout for that child should begin.

7. Consequences. A logical conclusion is frequently very powerful. Always connect the punishment to the wrongdoing.

8. Pick your battles. Choose the top four things you will not tolerate and concentrate on correcting them only for those four actions. This will show your child what is truly important to you while also avoiding the appearance that you are always punishing them.

9. Set boundaries. Try telling your kids what you are going to do or allow rather than telling them what to do. "When you have finished your chores, I'll be pleased to take you to visit your friends".

10. Positively state what you're requesting. Ever notice how we almost always ask for something or provide instructions in the negative? What they cannot have is the first thing your child hears. Your youngster will cooperate more if you simply alter the format of your requests. Try to frame the situation positively by telling them what they can have or what you will permit.

When you are dictating to them what they can have or what you would permit, they are less likely to dispute it.

4.2 Take Advantage of every Opportunity to Talk about your Feelings and the Conditions that Cause Them

According to studies, young children who have the opportunity to discuss the causes and effects of emotions acquire more emotional competence. See these empathy-building strategies for more details later in this chapter.

Tips for instilling empathy in youngsters that are backed up by research

Is it possible to teach empathy? Yes.

However, having a good role model isn't enough to teach empathy.

It requires more than simply allocating children to a few instructional activities.

We must comprehend the psychology of empathy, as well as the fundamental skills that children require to exchange feelings, read minds, and offer assistance.

Is it possible to teach empathy? If you think of empathy as an innate, fixed trait — a talent that some people are born with and others are not — this may seem bizarre.

But empathy isn't a one-size-fits-all approach. It is not something that occurs on its own in every circumstance. It's not even a single skill or ability.

According to researchers, "empathy" has become a catch-all term for at least three distinct processes:

- feeling another person's emotions (e.g., if you're scared, it makes me scared);

- reasoning about another person's perspective (e.g., you "put yourself in my shoes" and try to imagine what I'm thinking or feeling); and

- wanting to help — feeling sympathy and concern for someone who is vulnerable or distressed.

And learning has an impact on all of these processes.

Take, for example, the ability to sense another person's emotions. This trait, dubbed "affective empathy," appears to be instinctive and basic. It appears to exist in newborns and a variety of non-human animals.

But that does not dismiss the possibility that learning has an impact on the development of emotional empathy.

Your baby, for example, may be distressed because he/she hears another baby crying. Is he, however, capable of sharing all of your feelings?

No. He/she hasn't yet figured out how to read all of your facial expressions. He/she hasn't yet grasped the whole variety of emotions that can be felt or the events that cause them.

A child's development of affective empathy is influenced by a variety of factors, including how people communicate with him/her, the kind of social relationships he/she has, and if we help him/her cope with unpleasant or overpowering shared feelings.

Similarly, other empathetic processes can be stated to be similar.

To understand another person's point of view, you must first understand his/her universe.

To express sympathy, you must understand what the other person needs. You can also require a sense of justification that the other person deserves. A child's ideas regarding which types of people deserve empathy are shaped by cultural pressures such as authoritative figures and the popular media.

So empathy isn't something you have or don't have, and it isn't something that develops naturally without environmental involvement.

It's important to have personal experience. Culture is important. Parenting is important.

Here are a few pointers for guiding children on the right route.

Tip #1 for teaching empathy: Give youngsters the assistance they need to develop strong self-control.

It's difficult to feel another person's pain, so it's understandable if a child's first reaction is to withdraw. It's a natural, self-defense response.

However, in order to become compassionate helpers rather than bystanders, children must learn to manage this inclination. And we may assist in a variety of ways.

To begin, we can assist by practicing "positive parenting," which is a compassionate, responsive style to child-rearing that gives children a sense of security.

The benefits of sensitive, responsive parenting have been proven by decades of research.

It gives youngsters the impression that they can rely on us for emotional and physical assistance, resulting in stronger and more stable social ties. What happens when children feel safe? When they sense someone in need of sympathy and assistance, they are more willing to take emotional risks and get engaged.

Second, we may assist children by teaching them positive ways to deal with their own unpleasant emotions.

Children who are better at managing their negative emotions are more likely to exhibit empathy for others. As a result, it makes sense to provide "emotion coaching" to children.

This entails recognizing (rather than ignoring) negative emotions and engaging children in discussions about the sources and effects of emotions.

It also entails assisting children in developing constructive coping mechanisms for their negative emotions.

Emotion coaching has been shown to benefit children of all ages in studies. However, younger children who suffer from negative emotions may be the most benefited.

So, if you're a parent of a toddler, it's never too early to consider your job as an emotion coach. Parents who were encouraged to boost their coaching efforts had immediate, favorable results in one study. The ability of preschoolers to deal with frustration has improved.

Tip #2 Understand how feelings of shame and guilt can alter a child's empathic responses

Consider the following scenario: a child and his elder brother.

The child is sobbing. He slipped and fell, injuring his knee. He's bleeding and appears to be in a lot of pain.

Sam, the oldest brother, is keeping an eye on things. Is he compassionate? Is he attempting to assist his little brother?

It depends on the situation.

Assume the child was knocked off his feet by a rambunctious dog.

In this instance, Sam will very certainly feel empathy and express it. He'll treat his younger brother with compassion.

But what if Sam is to blame for the toddler's mishap?

It could have happened by chance. Or perhaps the older brother got enraged and lost his cool for a brief minute. In any case, he contributed to his younger brother's injury.

Things have become more complicated since then. Sam's reactions include thoughts about himself and his actions. And these self-conscious feelings can obstruct empathic responses.

If Sam thinks that he's the "bad guy" — or that other people perceive him as the "bad guy" — he'll be less likely to express empathy.

We don't normally respond in a constructive or prosocial way when we're ashamed — or when we're the subject of shaming methods.

We tend to feel helpless if we admit our shame. We either hide or sulk. We tend to feel bitter and furious if we reject the humiliation leveled at us. We're going all-in. Perhaps even lash out. This is supported by decades of research. Shame does not transform us into better individuals. It doesn't compel us to help victims. It causes people to act in careless or even hostile ways.

When Sam feels guilty, on the other hand, he is more inclined to exhibit empathy and want to make amends.

Shame is not the same as guilt. When we're feeling guilty, we think about our poor decisions and, more importantly, the hurt we've done to others.

As a result, guilt motivates us to take productive action. We don't feel helpless in any way. We are neither resentful nor furious. We are saddened by other people's suffering and desire to help them. We must avoid feelings of shame if we want our children to respond to these situations with empathy. We shouldn't label Sam as wicked just because he appears unrepentant or unfeeling.

We must not confront him in such a way that he feels threatened or degraded.

Instead, we should draw his attention to the implications of his actions, speak with him about his brother's feelings, and assist him in making amends.

Tip #3 for teaching empathy: Take advantage of everyday opportunities to activate your child's empathy mode.

Children show an ability to empathize from an early age. However, they, like us, do not always use it. So, how can you teach a child to empathize with others?

According to research, all we have to do is ask. A simple question, such as asking children to consider how other people are feeling, can have a big impact.

A researcher and her colleagues, for example, presented a hypothetical circumstance regarding a classmate to over 400 Dutch schoolchildren (aged 4 - 8 years) in an experiment.

Half of the pupils were instructed to act as though the classmate was a buddy. Half of the class was instructed to pretend that the classmate was not a personal friend. And the situation was as follows: it was your turn to stay late and clean up the classroom, and it was your classmate's turn to do so too. He/She does, however, want to return home as soon as possible because his/her mother is ill. He/she requests your assistance. Would you go through with it or would you help him/her?

What did the youngsters have to say?

It was all about friendship. When the female was not depicted as a friend, the children were less ready to help.

However, when researchers added an extra phase to the method, which required children to pause and ponder, the results altered. Instead of asking children right away if they wanted to help, the researchers had them think about the girl and rate how unhappy or upset she was likely to feel.

The children showed no prejudice in favor of the friend after assessing emotions. Whether the female was a friend or not, they were as likely to say they would assist her. The additional reminder was enough to sway the children's opinions.

Tip #4 Teaching empathy: Assist children in identifying what they have in common with others.

When adults see someone who is similar to them, they are more likely to feel empathy for them. They can also relate more easily with someone they know.

According to the study, children exhibit similar biases.

As a result, making youngsters aware of what they have in common with others is one of the finest strategies to develop empathy.

According to studies, schools that promote multiculturalism — an accepting, loving attitude toward ethnic variety — increase empathy among children.

Tip #5 for teaching empathy: Don't shield your youngster from race conversations. Discuss racial biases and injustices freely.

This piece of advice is especially important for white parents. Many white parents have a "color blind" approach to race, refusing to acknowledge the existence of racial classifications.

The color blind technique, they hope, will prevent children from forming racial biases. However, the evidence does not support this optimism. Children, on the other hand, imbibe racial biases through popular culture, whether we talk about it or not.

Furthermore, research reveals that when parents take a "race conscious" approach, identifying and addressing the presence of race and racism, white children become less biased.

As a result, confronting race is a vital aspect of teaching empathy.

People have a lower level of empathy for persons they believe to be different. We can offset this effect by assisting children in discovering the commonalities they share with others. Race, on the other hand, has a devastating effect on empathy. People aren't merely biased in favor of their in-groups.

Racist myths and prejudices also have an impact on people. For example, in the United States, researchers have found a weird but alarmingly prevalent racist myth: People are biased in thinking that black people experience less pain than white people.

This implicit assumption has been observed in both black and white persons, and it first appears in childhood. A researcher discovered that by the age of ten, children had developed a strong and consistent prejudice.

Regardless of their other beliefs about race or their experiences with interracial contact, the children, like their adult counterparts, have this bias. So having good intentions isn't going to make it go away. To dispel this notion, we must discuss it honestly and explicitly.

Tip #6 Understanding the value of perspective-taking and nurturing this type of empathy through practice exercises and group discussion is teaching empathy.

When we think about empathy, we usually think of affective empathy or sharing another person's feelings.

It's understandable that this emphasis is placed on it. Emotional intimacy appears to be built on the foundation of affective empathy. However, there is a price to pay.

Sharing another person's feelings can make us feel uncomfortable, especially when we're dealing with someone who is in pain or sorrow. It can also act as a reference for distraction. We become absorbed with our own emotional problems rather than paying attentive attention to the requirements of the other person. As a result, simply feeling affective empathy isn't adequate. We also need something psychologists call "cognitive empathy" to be good helpers: the ability to understand another person's perspective and appropriately recognize what that person requires. The procedure is more detached and cerebral, as well as less stressful. It also leads to more precise decisions. Individuals who score high in cognitive empathy have decreased stress reactivity when they encounter others' misery, according to brain scan research.

They're also better at replying in a helpful manner. So, how can we encourage cognitive empathy? Emotional coaching is a good place to start.

Games and activities that encourage children to consider how other people feel, think, want, and need them are also beneficial.

For example, researchers at the University of Wisconsin-Madison designed and tested the Kindness Curriculum, a 12-week school program.

It includes group lectures on paying attention to one's own and others' emotions, practical brainstorming sessions for assisting others, and thankfulness exercises for toddlers. The program was proven to be helpful for teaching empathy and preschool social skills in randomized, controlled research.

Tip #7: Assist young toddlers in developing their face-reading abilities.

If you can't read people's faces properly, it's difficult to demonstrate empathy.

Because they misinterpret facial emotions, some children, particularly toddlers, are at a disadvantage. These children misidentify what they see when you show them images of individuals modeling various emotions (happy, sadness, anger, fear, surprise, and contempt). Their difficulties can also lead to social issues.

Tip #8: When kids are trying to envision how someone else feels, show them how to "create a face."

Assume I instruct you to make a sorrowful face. Or a joyful expression. Alternatively, an enraged scowl. I mean, it's just a game, right? No, not at all.

Experiments have shown that simply "going through the motions" of generating a facial expression can cause us to feel the emotion it represents.

When volunteers were instructed to emulate various facial expressions, researchers noticed changes in brain activity that are associated with those emotions. People's heart rates, skin conductance, and body temperature also alter in response to their emotions.

As a result, research shows that we can improve our empathy by emulating the facial expressions of persons with whom we desire to empathize.

Tip #9: Assist children in developing a moral sense based on internal self-control rather than external rewards and punishments.

Kids are capable of being helpful and compassionate on the spur of the moment. Experiments have demonstrated that if children are rewarded financially for helping others, they are less inclined to do so.

According to other research, a punitive approach to punishment encourages youngsters to lie. Personal criticism and shaming tactics, as we've seen, frequently backfire.

So, how can we develop a child's moral compass?

We want youngsters to be able to self-regulate from the inside out. And studies show that when parents utilize inductive discipline, which emphasizes rational explanations and moral implications rather than arbitrary laws and harsh penalties, children are more likely to develop an internal sense of right and wrong.

When parents communicate to their children about how wrongdoing affects others, for example, they are more likely to acquire moral ideals.

Tip #10: Explain the "hot-cold empathy divide" to children.

Everyone understands that prior experiences have an impact on empathy. It's difficult to comprehend what another person's suffering is like if you've never experienced it.

Even prior experience, however, is insufficient to establish empathy. Why? We forget because we are human.

The "hot-cold empathy gap," as researchers term it, appears to be a common flaw in the human mind.

It's easy to be "cool-headed" when we're safe, peaceful, and at ease. However, we have a difficult time recalling what it's like to be in the grasp of a "hot" psychological state. We can't remember exactly how it feels to be in pain. Or it could be hunger. Or it might be tiredness. Alternatively, you could be afraid. Or maybe it's rage. Alternatively, it could be a loss. Alternatively, you could be depressed.

This forgetting could be beneficial. It can assist us in recovering from traumatic events. However, it has the potential to impair our capacity to make sound decisions. You're less likely to prevent something from happening again if you don't recall how awful it was the first time!

It can also make it difficult for us to sympathize with others.

As a result, it's critical to teach children about the hot-cold empathy divide and how it might skew our judgments. Before you dismiss someone as unreasonable, consider this: Have you forgotten what it's like to be in his/her shoes?

Tip #11: Discuss with your children the justifications people use to excuse harsh or cruel behavior.

According to studies, ordinary, well-adjusted people can be convinced to injure others — even torture them — if they are given the correct justification.

Participants were informed they were taking part in a "learning experiment" that required them to give severe electrical stimulation to another person in a renowned set of experiments performed by Yale University's Stanley Milgram.

The "experiment" was a hoax aided by convincing props and an actor who seemed to be in pain when research participants touched a button. However, the volunteers were duped, and under the orders of an authoritative figure in a white lab coat, they duly shocked the screaming "victim."

Even after the "victim" looked to be unconscious, about 65 percent of participants continued to click the button.

These individuals were not psychopaths. They were regular folks who were subjected to peer pressure from a credible authority figure. Otherwise good persons can disengage their moral responses with the correct rationalizations. It's not only a phenomenon that affects adults. It is also possible for children to do so.

(4.2.1) Don't minimize or dismiss your Child's sentiments, and don't penalize him/her for expressing Negative Emotions

If your youngster is throwing a temper tantrum, it's best to take a step back and wait until the rage has subsided before intervening.

However, once your child has calmed down enough to listen, be prepared to discuss what he/she is experiencing. Some behaviors are unacceptable, and we must state this clearly. However, we must make it plain that we recognize and embrace our children's feelings.

4.3. Alternative Solutions for your Child when He/She is Upset or Sad

Discuss these practical ways for making friends with your child if he/she is having problems fitting in at school.

(4.3.1) Twelve evidence-based strategies for assisting children in making friends

How can we assist children in making friends? It may appear that we have limited options. After all, making friends is a very personal endeavor.

Building a friendship, on the other hand, is dependent on a child's emotional intelligence, self-control, and social competency. Parents, in particular, can play a vital role in the development of these skills. Many children, for example, struggle to make friends because they are shy or frightened. We can assist these kids in forming vital social relationships if we teach them how to respond to pleasant overtures and offer them convenient, safe opportunities to interact with kind adults.

Similarly, some youngsters suffer because they lack proper impulse control or act in ways that are disruptive to others. If we help these youngsters develop their self-control skills, it will be a lot simpler for them to make friends.

And almost every youngster will benefit from social arts coaching and practice. Successful friendship relies on the same core skills everywhere around the world. To be successful, children must be able to:

- regulate their own negative emotions;

- understand other people's emotions and perspectives;

- show sympathy and offer assistance to friends in need;

- feel secure and trusting of others;

- know how to handle introductions and participate in the conversation;

- be capable of cooperation, negotiation, and compromise;

It's a large list, and mastering these abilities takes time, effort, and practice.

Parents and instructors, on the other hand, can be quite beneficial. It isn't a magic trick to make friends. It's something we pick up along the way. Something that we can teach our children.

So here's a list of 12 actual ways we can help kids develop friends, based on research.

1. Be friendly and respectful to your youngster. Don't use threats, punishments, or emotional "blackmail" to try to control your child.

It may not appear to have an immediate bearing on your child's capacity to make friends.

However, how parents treat their children has an impact on their emotional and social development. This, in turn, may have an impact on their peer connections.

Consider authoritarian parenting, a method of child-rearing that emphasizes strict obedience, a lack of love, and the use of threats, punishments, or humiliation to regulate conduct.

Authoritarian parenting has been related to the development of behavior issues in studies conducted all over the world. Additionally, children with behavioral issues have a harder time finding friends.

It also appears that parental psychological control — the use of guilt trips, shame, or withdrawal of affection to manipulate children — sets children up for poor-quality connections.

Children become more prosocial over time when parents demonstrate warmth and employ good discipline tactics such as reasoning with children and discussing the reasons behind rules.

They are more prone to show compassion and kindness to others.

They are less aggressive, more self-sufficient, and more well-liked by their peers.

So, without resorting to threats and punishments, how can we ensure that good behavior is enforced?

2. Act as an "emotion coach" for your youngster.

Negative emotions and selfish inclinations are common in all of us. Does it make difficult for us to keep excellent friendships? No, if we know how to keep our reactions under check.

As a result, youngsters must learn to control their own emotions. And what about the parents? Either we can assist them, or we can make things more difficult for them.

In one study, for example, researchers asked moms of 5-year-olds how they dealt with their children's negative emotions. The researchers then followed the progress of the children for several years. What went wrong?

Kids who grew up with a parent who talked with them about how to manage negative moods and tough feelings – sympathetically and constructively — were more likely to acquire excellent self-regulation skills. And the greater a child's self-control skills were, the more likely he/she was to form favorable peer relationships as an adult. On the other hand, research shows that when parents disregard their children's negative emotions ("You're just being stupid!") or punish them ("Go to your room!"), children develop inferior self-regulation skills.

When children become upset, it's important to take the time to understand their sentiments and actively educate them on how to deal with them in a healthy, productive manner.

3. Encourage your child to sympathize and "read people's minds."

More than just controlling their own negative emotions is required of children. They must also be aware of other people's feelings and viewpoints.

Aren't these things meant to happen by themselves? Perhaps, but "naturally" does not imply "without encouragement or help."

There are specific things that parents and teachers may do to assist children in developing their emotional awareness.

4. Do you have a socially anxious child? Assist in creating a safe social atmosphere.

When children are worried, it is difficult for them to develop friends. But what are our options?

For socially anxious youngsters, sensitive and attentive parenting is very vital. They must be certain that we will be there for them when they require assistance. And, as I've mentioned, research shows that sensitive, responsive parenting aids in the development of stable attachment ties, which foster confidence and independence in children.

However, when children are suffering from severe anxiety, they require further assistance.

They see the world as particularly dangerous, and unless we address this, they're likely to have chronic emotional issues — issues that might obstruct the development of social skills and make it difficult for a youngster to establish friends. So, if your child has a lot of anxiety, talk to your pediatrician or a school counselor about your worries.

Cognitive-behavioral therapy, a technique aimed to retrain your child's misperceptions and over-reactive emotional responses, has been established by child psychologists as an effective treatment for clinical anxiety. However, take in mind the following: Threats can be extremely real at times. Your child may, for example, attend a school where aggressive behavior is frequent.

It's possible that your youngster is aware of peers or neighbors who have been victims of violence. Perhaps your child is the victim of bullying, harassment, or peer rejection.

If this is your child's position, it makes sense to do everything you can to ameliorate his/her surroundings. Taking steps to prevent violence, harassment, and bullying is part of this. However, it may also entail locating a new social outlet for your children, such as a club or playgroup, that is exceptionally friendly and secure.

5. Deal with your child's issues with aggressive or disruptive behavior.

Such behavior issues can be a significant social obstacle to forming friends. Peers who act aggressively are often avoided or shunned by children.

What will you do if your child has a problem with yelling or violent behavior?

6. Teach your child how to communicate effectively.

Kids must learn how to introduce themselves to others and think of proper things to say in order to create new friends.

They must also learn to listen well. They also need to learn how to give conversational feedback, which demonstrates that they understand what the other person is saying.

What are the best ways to develop these abilities?

At home, we may help by modeling appropriate communication skills and engaging our children in enjoyable, reciprocal dialogues. Furthermore, we can assist by actively teaching children what to do and say.

When we teach children the skill of "active listening," for example, they gain profit.

When a person shows that he/she is paying attention by making acceptable eye contact, positioning the body in the direction of the speaker, remaining silent, and responding appropriately verbally.

We can teach kids how to be great conversationalists by providing them with the following tangible advice:

- Share information about your "likes" and "dislikes" when starting a conversation with someone new.

- Avoid becoming an interviewer. Don't just pose queries.

- Don't be a conversation hog; provide information about yourself. Only respond to the question at hand when in conversation. Allow your companion to speak when you've finished.

7. Organize social events that promote collaboration rather than rivalry.

According to studies, children get along better when they participate in cooperative activities, which require them to work together toward a common objective. This is true in both scenarios, while in the classroom or youngsters are playing.

So, if your child is having social difficulties, it's usually a good idea to keep them away from competitive games until they improve their social abilities. If your child has a playdate, take away any toys or games that could cause a fight. For example, they advise parents to put away toy weapons as well as any other items that could cause rivalry or jealousy. If your child has a beloved possession that he/she refuses to share, it's better to keep it hidden until the playdate is over.

8. Teach your youngster how to deal with uncomfortable social situations.

Let's take a closer look at what I'm talking about.

Assume Sam, a little child, watches numerous children playing together. Sam wishes to join them, but he is unsure how to do so. What should he do in this situation?

Researchers gave this hypothetical scenario to moms of preschool children and asked for their input. The mothers who provided the best advice were also the mothers whose children exhibited the best social skills.

What did these wise mothers have to say about it?

- Keep an eye on what the other kids are doing before approaching them. What can you do in order to blend in?

- Participate in the game by accomplishing something useful. If your children are playing a restaurant game, for example, check if you can become a new customer.

- Don't be obnoxious, critical, or try to change the game's rules.

- Don't force yourself to participate if the other kids don't want you to. Simply take a step back and find something else to do.

It's sound counsel that we can give to our own children. And we shouldn't overlook the study's main message: When we assist children in developing concrete skills for dealing with challenging social situations, they benefit.

9. Teach children how to compromise and negotiate.

Kids must be able to think of nonviolent ways to resolve problems in order to form positive relationships with their classmates. They must be able to comprehend what other people require and desire, as well as anticipate the ramifications of certain acts.

Growing up with siblings gives children an advantage in developing these talents. They have numerous opportunities to practice negotiation.

However, you don't need siblings to gain good social skills, and all children, regardless of their family structure, benefit from some direction and teaching.

Role-playing exercises and activities that ask kids to come up with solutions to hypothetical social conflicts, according to studies, can help them improve their skills.

As a result, research shows that actively guiding youngsters through the process can help them become better social problem-solvers. Consider it a lesson opportunity the next time your child butts heads with someone else. Encourage your child to come up with a solution that is agreeable to both parties.

10. Teach your youngster how to apologize and express regret.

It can happen to anyone. We make mistakes. We make poor decisions. We damage others or make them feel bad. So, what's next? We tend to focus on our own unpleasant emotions when we are embarrassed or "canceled" for our blunders. We could feel humiliated, resentful, or even angry. And that isn't going to help us mend our social bonds. Not at all.

Consider what happens when we have a feeling of guilt. It's possible that feeling guilty is beneficial. We examine the impact of our actions on others. We feel sorry for our victims. It also motivates us to strive to undo the harm we've done.

When it comes to creating and retaining friends, the distinction is critical.

Children as young as four years old are more willing to forgive a peer for wrongdoing if that person actively apologizes, according to studies.

As children grow older (and smarter), they become more aware of indicators indicating the perpetrator is sorry. In fact, if people see symptoms of contrition, they don't usually want an outright apology.

But what's the best method to mend a broken relationship? Don't merely apologize or pretend to be sorry. Please make adjustments.

Researchers studied how children, aged 6 and 7 years old, reacted to a transgressor who knocked down a tower they'd been building.

Even if the transgressor apologized, the children were still offended. The only way these kids felt better was if the transgressor actively assisted them in re-constructing their tower.

So that's what we should strive for: teaching our children how to mend relationships and overcome negative emotions. We should teach children how to offer apologies and make amends for their faults from an early age.

11. Teach your youngster to be forgiving and understanding of others' errors.

Children can be forgiving, but it is not always a natural trait. In reality, some children struggle with vengeance on a regular basis. They have a tendency to believe that others are unfriendly, and they may ruminate over perceived slights and insults.

If that's your child's issue, you'll want to assist him/her in changing his/her perspective of others. Encourage your youngster to understand the perspective of a transgressor and to investigate other explanations for troublesome behavior.

Perhaps it was an unintentional mishap. Perhaps the transgressor was upset about something or was exhausted or sick. Maybe the transgressor was just having a bad day, and you got in his/her way.

Children are more likely to give perpetrators the due credit of the doubt when adults prompt them to consider alternate explanations.

Of course, not every youngster requires such encouragement. Some children are too forgiving to wrongdoers.

When they are victimized, they blame themselves and stay in relationships where they are constantly exploited or mistreated.

As a result, we must be aware of the situation and provide each child with the help he/she requires.

12. Keep an eye on your child's social life, but don't get too involved - especially as your youngster gets older.

Youngsters are better off when their parents are informed about their social activities, according to studies from many cultures.

This is known as "parental monitoring," and it entails things like:

- supervising where young children play;

- assisting children in finding opportunities to meet and socialize with friends, prosocial peers;

- conversing with your children's friends when they come to visit; and

- Ask your children to tell you about their free-time activities.

There's also evidence in support of enforcing specific boundaries, such as requiring your adolescent to inform you ahead of time about the circumstances of an evening out.

Who are you going to spend it with? What are your plans? What route will you take?

Parents, on the other hand, must exercise caution. By being too invasive, they can embarrass their children and scare away potential pals.

Kids are more inclined to reject our advice if they believe we are too controlling. In fact, if teenagers considered their parents were overstepping their authority, they were more likely to choose a delinquent peer as a companion, according to one study.

As a result, it's critical to give your child a sense of autonomy and to communicate your worries in a reasonable and polite manner. Otherwise, your youngster may begin to regard your authority as illegitimate and act out accordingly.

(4.3.2) Children's facial expressions: Assisting them in Reading Emotions

When attempting to interpret other people's emotions, you do not solely rely on their facial expressions. You make decisions based on a multitude of factors, including tone of voice, body language, and contextual cues.

Facial expressions, on the other hand, are quite significant. And what about your capacity to decipher them? They're tied to social, intellectual, and psychological results.

Children with better face-reading skills, for example, may be more popular at school. They have a stronger academic record. Furthermore, studies show that those who are better at recognizing terrified signs are more generous and caring.

Children who have difficulty recognizing emotion in faces, on the other hand, are more likely to have peer problems and learning challenges.

Preschoolers who have poor face-reading skills for their age are more prone to develop externalizing behavioral problems and engage in overt aggressiveness.

What if your child is extremely shy? Poor emotion recognition, according to research, can make it more difficult. Shy preschoolers with poor face-reading skills had higher levels of anxiety and peer rejection in one study.

So, what factors influence a child's ability to interpret faces?

It is important to be of a certain age. Researchers from all over the world, from Canada to the Netherlands to Italy to Japan, have confirmed that as youngsters become older, they become more accurate.

For example, we know that babies notice our facial expressions and can detect the difference between a pleasing smile and an angry grimace even at a young age. We also know that:

- Toddlers sympathize with people who appear distressed;
- 30-month-old children can correctly identify emojis that represent basic emotions; and
- 3-year-olds can correctly identify happy and angry faces about 80% of the time — as long as the facial expressions are fairly intense.

However, this does not imply that young children have a sophisticated ability to interpret all of the emotions expressed on a genuine, live face.

Face-reading skills, on the other hand, appear to develop throughout childhood and adolescence, with some emotions being acquired later than others.

Take, for example, two major emotions: happiness and rage. Researchers have discovered that 5-6 year old children can accurately identify both happy and angry faces in studies.

However, studies show that proper understanding of sad faces takes years longer, with children as young as ten misinterpreting sad facial expressions as afraid.

While children tend to achieve adult like skills for all three emotions (happy, anger, and sadness) by the age of 10, this may only be true for extremely severe facial expressions. Kids are substantially less accurate when others convey their sentiments with more nuanced expressions.

Furthermore, even at high intensities, some emotions are difficult to discern. Researchers discovered that children struggled to distinguish disgust or fear throughout puberty in one study.

Is ASD (autism spectrum disorder) a possibility? Isn't it true that children with ASD have a harder time interpreting faces correctly?

There is some evidence to back up this claim. Researchers examined the talents of 95 children with ASD and compared them to 60 years age and gender matched children in a control group in a recent study.

Children with ASD took a little longer to perceive facial emotions and were also less accurate at detecting fear.

The most significant difference across groups, however, was in low-intensity anger. Only 41% of the time, children with ASD correctly identified low-intensity rage (versus about 82 percent of the time for youngsters in the control group).

Is it true that girls can read facial expressions better than boys?

Again, there is some support for this theory, but the gender differences appear to be minor. In a study of 470 children aged 6-10, researchers discovered that females were slightly more accurate in detecting happiness, surprise, disgust, and rage. Fear and melancholy showed no gender differences.

What impact does culture have on a youngster's ability to read facial expressions?

Contrary to popular belief, not all people identify the same facial expressions, even for basic emotions like happiness and fear.

Researchers, for example, presented people with photos of various facial expressions.

The photographs came from an official collection used by psychologists to portray allegedly universal facial expressions, but people in these photos didn't always perceive the expressions in the way that psychologists predicted. So it's very obvious. Children must absorb culturally appropriate facial expression clues as they get older.

(4.3.3) What can we do to assist children in Reading Faces?

According to research, parents can have a significant impact on their children's development of emotion detection. Here are some suggestions based on research.

1. Be a "mind-minded" parent, one who engages children in in-depth discussions about emotions.

According to studies, exposing toddlers to an accurate, sensitive conversation about thoughts and feelings helps them develop superior "emotion-reading" skills. When their parents assist them in finding appropriate labels for the emotions they perceive, children develop superior emotion-reading skills. Parents can also aid by talking about the causes and effects of certain emotions.

2. Instruct children to examine the full circumstance and context when interpreting facial emotions.

We shouldn't expect children, particularly young children, to rely solely on facial clues. Face expressions may be deciphered by young toddlers using their grasp of the scenario. If they witness someone drop their ice cream cone, for example, they may envision how they would feel if it occurred to them.

3. Discuss not only facial expressions but also other forms of body language with your children.

Children are perceptive to a lot more than just a person's expressions. They also pay attention to the tone of a person's voice, their body posture, and their gestures.

Help youngsters create connections between different types of nonverbal cues whether you're reading a novel together or seeing someone in real life.

4. Play emotion identification games for more practice.

Researchers have created training programs in which children are asked to practice identifying the emotions expressed through facial expressions.

In one study, for example, researchers taught typically developing primary school pupils how to recognize and self-produce facial clues. Children's ability to discern emotions improved after only six half-hour sessions when compared to controls.

Is it possible to use the same ideas at home? One method is to put together a collection of photos and use them to make "feeling cards."

Alternatively, you might purchase cards that are specifically designed for this purpose. Picture by Picture, for example, sells a pack of 40 cards representing ten different moods as shown by a variety of faces.

What can you accomplish with the cards you have? Take a look at these games.

Imagining emotions and imitating faces

Facial mimicking isn't merely a theatrical practice. According to research, it also aids in the identification of emotions and the sense of empathy. As an example, consider the following: Shuffle the deck and lay the cards face down.

The first player chooses a card, keeps it to herself, and then imitates the card's expression. The other player(s) must guess which emotion is being expressed.

Face-to-situation matching

You'll need a deck of cards for this game, each illustrating an emotional circumstance. After that, players must match each facial expression card to the most relevant context.

Your situation cards' graphics might come from a variety of places. You can either draw your own or clip out images from magazines. Some situation cards can elicit a range of emotions.

What's the deal with that face?

In this simple game, players take turns drawing a card from the deck and inventing a rationale for the facial expression depicted. If the player chooses a card with a woman looking shocked, you can respond, "She just found a dinosaur in her bathtub."

A game based on a child psychology technique that encourages collaborative, improvised storytelling.

Technique used by psychologists to get young children to talk about and picture particular themes and concepts, such as separation from loved ones, peer conflict, and moral difficulties.

The psychologist creates a hypothetical circumstance and asks the youngster to fill in the blanks about what occurs next. In this cooperative game, participants can choose the fundamental scenario together.

It can be fantastical, but it must feature characters that have authentic emotional responses. The participants then work together to develop a story, taking turns and expanding on one other's ideas.

To start, the first player chooses an emotion card and begins the story. He/she can choose any direction he/she wants with the story, but he must include the emotion depicted on the card — that is, events in the story must reflect the proper feeling. The next player takes a turn picking a card and continuing the story, and so on. Players continue to take rounds until all of the cards have been used, or a satisfactory ending has been reached.

4.4 Instill a Positive, Constructive Attitude

If children believe they are "bad," they may believe they are powerless to change. As a result, it's critical for children to understand that practice makes perfect. Taking a proactive strategy to address your child's faults is one way to transmit this lesson.

The golden words that help kids cope with mistakes are "correcting behavior."

Children can be disappointing at times. They make mistakes, misbehave, or just do not live up to our expectations. What will be the correct way of dealing with these setbacks? You could be honest with your children and tell them how you feel. "You have let me down."

However, experiments show that this is not the optimal strategy.

Personal critique, on the other hand, can be construed as a judgment about a person's inherent limitations.

Children may take words like "you're such a slacker" or "I'm disappointed in you" to heart. They may lead to the realization that they are inherently inferior and feel powerless to change. They make no attempt to develop themselves or learn from their failures.

"You are behaving lazy," rather than "you are lazy," is a better way to refer to a child's behavior.

But what's the most effective technique to get results? Do you want to change your habits? Is it possible to motivate children to do better?

Decades of research have all pointed to the same conclusion. When we focus on rewarding what they've done well rather than penalizing what they've done incorrectly, kids are more likely to progress.

According to studies, the correct kind of praise — commending a child's efforts, methods, or good deeds — can motivate children to keep striving.

This form of praise, known as "process praise," has been connected to positive child outcomes, including academic ones.

But, what should you do if your child makes a mistake?

When they've made a mistake, don't add to the embarrassment. Instead, teach your youngster to approach problems in a problem-solving manner. Encourage your youngster to come up with solutions.

This is supported by a fascinating experiment conducted on kindergarten students.

"Can you think of a better solution?"

These could be the magic words, as we'll see later.

What happens when we criticize children who are still young?

Here is a story that is being related to a group of young children.

You're playing with Legos one day. Mrs. Bill, the instructor, approaches and asks, "Will you build me a magnificent house out of those Legos?"

"OK, Mrs. Bill," you say. So you put forth a lot of effort to construct a good home for the teacher. You build four walls out of Legos and then add a roof on top. You really want to build Mrs. Bill a wonderful house, but as you look down at the one you created, you realize, "Uh-oh, I forgot to put any windows on the house," but you still want to offer it to her, so you say, "Teacher, I built a house for you!" "That house has no windows," the teacher remarks, pointing to the house you created.

There were four possible conclusions to the story.

- There was no further action in the control condition. The teacher remarked on the lack of windows but didn't say anything else.

- The story finished with the teacher's disapproval in the Person Criticism condition. She delivered a number of remarks before concluding, "I'm disappointed in you."

- The teacher's criticism in the Outcome Criticism condition was directed at the outcome rather than the child. "That's not the way to go about it."

- In the Process Criticism condition, the teacher merely pointed out the error ("The blocks are all twisted and in one huge mess") and then encouraged the student to consider other options: "Perhaps you might think of another way to do it."

Interviewers asked kids a variety of questions when the narrative ended, such as:

- How did the story make you feel?

- Did you feel like a nice girl or a bad girl after reading the story?

- Did you feel smart or stupid after reading the story?

The students were also put to the test in terms of their perseverance. The kids were instructed to create their own sequel to the story by the interviewers. What would the protagonist's child do next?

"Would you prefer to do the Lego house again or do something else instead?" the youngsters were asked.

The children reacted to the various types of feedback, one of them is in the following way:

Children who had received personal criticism ("I'm disappointed in you") were more likely to believe they weren't competent at the scenario's skill.

They were less confident in themselves and were more prone to give up without resolving the issue.

Parenting in everyday situations

These investigations, of course, were focused on a child's architectural efforts rather than behavioral issues. Is it possible to apply the notion of process feedback to the types of misbehavior that most parents face?

I believe so, but we must bear this in mind. Kids frequently get into problems for reasons they don't fully comprehend. To resolve a quarrel, they turn to violence. Or they disobey the rules we've established for them. Alternatively, they act in a disruptive manner.

We must also assist them in determining what solutions are available.

It's critical for young children, for example, to talk with us about how their actions affect others. Youngsters' perspective-taking abilities are still developing in young children. They don't always know how to make other people feel better, and they don't always know how to anticipate how others will react.

What about public shaming? Is it always a terrible idea to do so? As we've seen, the researchers' tests didn't involve youngsters who were disobedient, greedy, or purposefully disruptive. Could the phrase "I'm disappointed in you" be helpful in such situations? Isn't it true that making children feel ashamed would inspire them to behave better?

The evidence contradicts this.

When we are shamed, as I already stated, we feel tremendously threatened. As a result, we may get enraged and bitter, or we may attempt to absolve ourselves of responsibility for our actions.

And, as we saw in the kindergartner study, guilt can make children feel powerless to change. Simply put, I'm a bad person. I can't do anything about it.

Then there are the issues that come when youngsters are publicly shamed. It's one thing to quietly express your dissatisfaction with a child's behavior. Another is exposing his/her flaws to the rest of the world.

According to research involving young primary school students, kids are more inclined to reject peers who they perceive to be in less supportive student-teacher interactions.

When pupils are singled out for being inept or misbehaving, the other students in the class are less likely to accept them socially.

Needless to say, this is harmful, and not just because it isolates children socially. Children who feel rejected by their peers are less motivated at school, which can lead to reduced success, increased behavior problems, and even more social rejection.

Does this imply that we should avoid discussing the repercussions of children's misbehavior with them?

Obviously not. Shame and guilt are two different emotions, according to psychologists. Guilt causes us to focus on the people we've wronged. It makes us want to make amends. To rectify the situation, it is, in essence, a socially beneficial emotion.

It is our conscience that pushes us to be better. Should we tell them that their actions are unacceptable? Yes. Should we ask children to think about the victims' feelings? Yes. Empathy is a crucial component of moral growth. However, we can accomplish these goals without making children feel hopeless or degraded.

More information about behavior correction can be found here.

Criticism is just one method to make children feel powerless in the face of their failures. Another option is to lavish children with inappropriate praise. Generic praise ("You're very smart!") has been shown to lead children to believe that intelligence is an innate, fixed trait and that accomplishment is influenced by variables outside their control, according to research. As a result, when these children fail, they give up quickly. Children may lose motivation if they believe praise is given in a fake or undeserved manner.

Chapter 5

Authoritarian Parenting

5.1 What happens to Children when their Parents are Authoritarian?

The authoritarian parenting style emphasizes sternness and strictness. It demands complete obedience and enforces excellent behavior by psychological manipulation, such as threats, humiliation, and other forms of punishment.

It's also a style associated with less parental warmth and responsiveness, according to psychologists. That isn't good news for children's health, especially under stressful situations. Warmth and responsiveness can help children avoid the negative consequences of toxic stress.

But what about the other possibilities? Do you like the outcomes when it comes to behavioral issues? What are your social skills? What are your academic achievements? Shouldn't their children be better behaved and more successful in the classroom if their parents are demanding?

Surprisingly, the research suggests the opposite. Here's a quick rundown of the findings.

Alternatives to authoritarianism

At least three alternatives to authoritarian parenting have been identified by researchers:

- Permissive parents are extremely warm, but they are hesitant to impose rules or standards of behavior.
- Parents who are uninvolved are similar to permissive parents, but they lack warmth.

- Authoritative parents, like authoritarian parents, establish boundaries and enforce rules. Authoritative parents, on the other hand, are more responsive and nurturing than authoritarian parents.

Furthermore, authoritative parents encourage their children to ask questions and explain why rules are in place.

Authoritative parents are also less prone to use shame, guilt, or the withdrawal of love to exert control over their children.

What does authoritarianism have to offer?

Problems with behavior

There's a growing body of data that harsh techniques harm children.

When children exhibit particularly challenging behavior, it may appear that the only solution is strict discipline – the use of threats, harsh punishments, or humiliation to keep youngsters under control. However, evidence suggests that these strategies do not lead to long-term behavioral changes. On the contrary, they appear to aggravate the situation.

Consider disruptive, aggressive, belligerent, or antisocial behavior, which psychologists refer to as "externalizing behavior issues." We should expect fewer such behavior problems as children become older if authoritarian discipline approaches are effective. When we track children's development, though, we don't see that.

Researchers discovered that harsh control and psychological control were the largest predictors of worsened behavior over time in a meta-analysis of over 1400 published studies. Children who were subjected to these authoritarian approaches at one point in time tended to suffer greater externalizing behavior problems later on.

Why?

It's impossible to say that it's totally attributable to authoritarian parenting. Perhaps hereditary factors have a role. After all, we know that certain hereditary variables can increase a child's likelihood of having behavioral issues.

This type of youngster may elicit authoritarian attitudes from their carers. Parents struggle to find a solution when their children misbehave. They are irritated and anxious. They punish their wayward children with strong discipline - threats and penalties — and show less warmth toward them.

It's a scenario in which behavior problems are linked to authoritarian parenting, but not because authoritarian parenting causes behavior problems. Instead, the children play a role in the story. Authoritarian attitudes are triggered by their misbehavior.

So, how do we figure out what's going on here? Researchers have confirmed that children's pre-existing behavior problems can definitely prompt authoritarian reactions from parents when they try to separate apart its causes. There is evidence that authoritarianism is bad. It appears to exacerbate children's behavioral issues.

Researchers focused on children with "callous unemotional features," such as low empathy and weak moral self-regulation, in a behavioral genetics study.

These characteristics are linked to major behavioral issues, and the research team confirmed that genes play a role. Some children were more likely to develop "callous unemotional qualities" due to their genetic makeup.

However, parenting style had an impact as well. Children were less prone to develop callous-unemotional qualities when their parents showed them a lot of love and compassion. Even children with a high genetic risk had fewer signs and symptoms.

What about other kinds of misbehavior? Adolescent substance abuse, perhaps?

The evidence is alarming yet again. According to research, children with authoritarian parents are more prone to consume and abuse alcohol.

Resourcefulness and social skills

What impact does authoritarian parenting have on social skill development?

Children from authoritarian homes tend to have inferior social skills in a range of cultures around the world.

Examples?

Teenagers with authoritarian parents were shown to be the least likely to feel socially accepted by their peers in studies of American teenagers. They were also judged to be less self-sufficient.

Furthermore, a study of college students in the United States indicated that students reared by authoritarian parents were more prone to engage in bullying behavior.

Teachers in China evaluated children from authoritarian households as less socially adept in a survey of 2nd graders in Beijing. They were also less likely to be welcomed by their peers and were more hostile. Other Chinese studies have linked authoritarianism's punitive characteristics to lower social functioning.

Bullying has been connected to authoritarian parenting in Cyprus. When researchers polled 230 young teenagers about their cultural beliefs and peer experiences, they discovered that youngsters from authoritarian homes were more likely to have been victims and perpetrators of bullying.

Children from authoritarian homes were found to be less resourceful than children from permissive families in a study of Turkish high school students.

Spain and South America

Authoritarian parents are more likely to raise children with low social competence, according to researchers in Latin cultures, and the impacts may endure into adulthood.

A Spanish study also discovered a correlation between authoritarian parenting and bullying. Bullying was more common among high school kids whose parents were authoritarian, especially if their parents tried to control them through harsh discipline.

The Netherlands

In a Dutch study teachers and classmates assessed children with authoritarian parents as less helpful and popular. They were also judged to be less advanced in their moral reasoning.

5.2 Emotional Issues

Is authoritarian parenting more likely to cause emotional disorders in children? Yes, perhaps.

Adolescents from authoritarian homes, for example, had poorer self-esteem than adolescents from authoritative, "indulgent," or permissive families in Spain, Portugal, and Brazil. Adults in Spain who were reared by strict, authoritarian parents report lower levels of pleasure and life satisfaction.

In Germany, authoritarian parenting has been associated with a higher chance of developing depressive symptoms in children, as well as a higher risk of developing depressive symptoms in the United States and the Caribbean.

Kids who thought their parents were dictatorial were more likely to have mental health issues. Even after accounting for the influence of genes, researchers discovered, in a behavioral genetics study of Chinese twins, that children with authoritarian fathers were more likely to suffer from a psychiatric disease.

According to other research conducted in China, children who have severe parents have a harder time controlling their emotions.

In a Taiwanese study, children who thought their parents were authoritarian were more likely to have mental health problems.

Meanwhile, research in the United States and the Caribbean shows that when parents use an authoritarian style to child upbringing, their teenagers are more likely to develop depressive symptoms.

According to a behavioral genetics study, authoritarian parenting puts children at a higher risk of developing serious depression.

However, authoritarian parenting isn't always associated with emotional issues.

Some studies of adolescents in the United States have found no emotional differences between children raised in authoritarian, authoritative, or permissive households.

Furthermore, research on Middle Eastern adolescents has failed to uncover a link between authoritarian caregiving and psychological issues such as depression.

Why are there so many contradictions?

The effects of authoritarianism, I believe, are influenced by how harsh, frigid, or punitive the parent is. According to several studies, corporal punishment is associated with a higher incidence of depression and anxiety in youngsters. It's also possible that culture plays a part. Children may be less upset by authoritarianism if they see it as usual and mainstream.

What about going to school?

According to research, authoritarian approaches to learning impede learning.

In an interesting study of kindergartners, researchers discovered that a common authoritarian caregiving strategy — scolding a child for poor performance — can cause children to perform worse on problem-solving activities.

Furthermore, studies show that positive feedback helps people learn better than negative feedback, which may be especially true for children.

Other research has found a link between authoritarianism and worse academic achievement.

In a study of teenagers in the San Francisco Bay Area, for example, authoritarian parenting was connected to lower school grades across all ethnic groups. Other research that has come to similar conclusions back up these findings.

Evidence to the contrary: Is it true that when parents are less educated, the impacts are less harmful? Or do you live in a low-income area? Or is it Chinese?

Some studies of children from low-income homes found no difference in academic achievement between authoritative and authoritarian families.

It's even been stated that children from authoritarian households perform better in school than children from less-educated parents.

In traditional Chinese households, there is significant debate over the implications of authoritarian caregiving. On the one hand, in Beijing and Taiwan, authoritarianism has been associated with lower educational achievement.

Authoritarian parenting, on the other hand, has been associated with higher academic accomplishment in studies of Hong Kong and Chinese immigration to North America.

What's the deal with the discrepancies?

Several theories have been proposed by researchers.

It's possible that teaching unquestioning obedience to children in hazardous, underprivileged neighborhoods reduces their chances of running afoul of authority figures in and out of school.

Perhaps the impacts of parenting are overshadowed by peer pressure. Some peer groups encourage students to succeed in school. Others are opposed to it. Asian Americans tended to have peer networks that supported scholarship, and they performed well in school even when their parents were authoritarian, according to a survey of U.S. school pupils. Peer groups among African Americans tended to reject good students. Even when their parents were authoritarian and well-educated, their children performed worse in school. In different cultures, authoritarian parenting can signify different things. The Chinese style of authoritarian parenting, according to Ruth Chao, is fundamentally different. Chinese authoritarian parents have closer bondings or relationships with their children than Western authoritarian parents, and proximity is a predictor of higher academic accomplishment. But I'm not convinced that authoritarian parenting may help certain children become better students.

The results of the experimental investigation are compelling. Furthermore, critical thinking is required for success in math, science, and many other academic fields—something that authoritarian parenting appears to impede.

There is evidence that schools that operate on authoritarian principles produce lower-performing children. Researchers discovered that authoritative schools had the best results in a study comparing American high schools. Dropout rates were highest in authoritarian schools.

And what about morality?

Authoritarian parents may consider themselves moral crusaders. However, research shows that children raised by authoritarian parents are less managed in terms of self-control and moral thinking. Furthermore, as children grow older, children from authoritarian families may be more likely to "tune out" their parents.

For example, during the course of an 18-month study in the United States, researchers discovered that kids who identified their parents as more authoritarian were more likely to reject their parents as legitimate authority figures. Over time, they were also more prone to engage in delinquency.

In a survey of American undergraduates, researchers inquired about who they sought advice from when faced with moral dilemmas. Graduate students with authoritative parents were the most likely to say they would speak with their parents.

Kids with authoritarian parents were more likely to refer to their peers than students from permissive families.

5.3 Set Tough Boundaries while Maintaining Goodwill

Tips for dealing with situations as they crop up:

- Don't give in. When your child throws a tantrum, resist the urge to give in and give him/her what he/she wants. Giving in tells him/her that temper tantrums are effective.

- Maintain your composure. Harsh or emotional responses, whether verbal or physical, tend to aggravate a child's hostility. You're also modeling the type of conduct you want to see in your youngster by remaining calm.

- Praise positive behavior while ignoring undesirable behavior. Ignore small disobedience since even negative reinforcement, such as reprimanding or asking the child to stop, can reinforce his/her conduct. Instead, provide lots of labeled praise to the behaviors you'd like to see more of.

- Use consistent repercussions. Your child needs to understand the repercussions of bad behavior, such as time outs, as well as the benefits for good behavior, such as iPad time. And you must demonstrate to him/her that you always carry out these consequences.

- Don't say anything until the meltdown is over. When a child is distressed, don't try to reason with them. When he/she isn't blowing up (and you aren't either), you want to encourage him/her to try negotiating.

Specific behaviors are being targeted

It's helpful to pinpoint specific habits that you're seeking to change while dealing with disruptive behavior (or encouragement). It's true that when a family is stressed, every contact can feel like a battle.

Identifying particular behaviors, on the other hand, is a vital first step in a successful discipline. Taking each behavior one at a time allows you to focus better, obtain a better knowledge of why the behavior is occurring, and feel more in control. Of course, you may want to change a number of behaviors, but it's critical to assess each one separately.

The following behaviors should be targeted:

- Particulars (so expectations are clear to everyone in the family)

- Observable

- Quantifiable (so everyone can agree whether or not the behavior happened)

"Acting out" or "being good" are two examples of poorly defined behaviors. Running around the room (poor) or starting schoolwork on time are examples of well-defined behaviors (good).

Conclusion

What should you do if a young child refuses to wash his/her teeth? yells while seated in the car, pinches the infant and won't eat his/her food and vegetables, throws books in a library room, goes amok in a grocery store? This book is a fundamental manual of communication techniques, organized by typical difficulties and disputes. With the help of this approachable manual, parents and other caregivers of young kids will be able to establish satisfying, joyful relationships with truly awful two-year-olds, querulous three-year-olds, fierce four-year-olds, reckless five-year-olds, self-centered six-year-olds, and the infrequent semi-civilized seven-year-olds. Also, it will help young kids grow up to be independent big kids who can work with their teachers, parents, friends, and siblings and keep in touch with them.

Useful Tips for Parents and Guardians

1. How can you resolve conflicts with your kids?

There are methods for encouraging children to cooperate. That is crucial. It always comes down to how you feel. If you don't feel right, it's likely that you won't act properly either. Problem-solving is a useful skill. Even if they have a tantrum, you can still go back and re-establish contact with your child. You are demonstrating a way of life; what should we do in the event of a disagreement? Do you consider a means to harm someone when they do something you don't like, such as slapping them? Or come up with a plan to make them endure a little pain, like locking them in their room without dessert.

Or do you converse with them, hear what they have to say, and work together to find a solution? That goes far further than simply telling your child what to do at a certain moment.

2. Parents frequently feel that their children are not paying attention or listening to them.

We adults have such a deep interest in topics that children do not. We are time obsessives; we rush out of the home to avoid being late; young children couldn't care about time. We have a cleaning obsession. Kids don't mind having sticky hair or being smelly; we want the kid with the smelly hair to get in the bathtub. Children are content to live in chaos; we want them to pick up after themselves. Therefore, there is a genuine disparity in needs and perceptions.

3. What is a rapid technique parents or guardians can use to get children to do something?

If an adult can be playful, children adore them. Making an inanimate thing speak is one method. If you can animate the sock and say, "I feel so flat and empty, won't someone stick a wonderful warm foot in me?" when trying to put a sock on for your 3-year-old, wouldn't that be better? The young child is suddenly thrilled to place his/her foot into the sock. The ambiance has altered. We are cooperating rather than fighting. We're doing it by playing.

4. What other method can parents employ?

Instead of a directive or command, offer an option. You may say, "How do you want to go to the car?" instead of, "Hurry, we're going to be late." Do you like to walk backward or forwards?

Do you want to wear roller skates or hop like a kangaroo? A child may act more cooperatively when given a small choice rather than a small directive or command.

5. Why not simply request that the child put their jacket away or stop complaining?

Let's say your partner greets you when you get home from work by saying, "Oh, good, you're home." Get your coat off, hang it up, and settle down to enjoy your meal. Did you hear me when I told you to sit down? 'Hurry up'.

There is a part of you that will resist even if the food smells delicious and you are sleepy since no one likes to be told what to do. Children who are constantly told what to do exhibit the same resentment as adults do.

6. Parents might feel too worn out to deal with the hassle.

You're working for the benefit of society. It's not as difficult as it seems. Once you start doing things like this, you'll notice that both you and your kids are enjoying life a little bit more. You're navigating the day with fewer conflicts and more enjoyment and positive emotions. What first appears to be extra work will actually make your life easier.

7. Some parents might think that other parents are performing better than they are.

We are confined to our small nuclear families and are unaware of the type of problems that exist. Everyone believes that their child is the only one who loses it when asked to draw four objects that begin with the letter B. However, children are sobbing uncontrollably throughout the community over their kindergarten assignments.

In our book, we attempt to recreate that sense of community so that you can get a glimpse into the lives of all the parents who are tackling the same problems in the same fallible, human way.

8. Words of wisdom for frustrated mothers

You occasionally need to give yourself some alone time. Say, I realize that you want me to stare at your photo and you need this, but I'm sorry, I'm unable to do that at this time. I need to sit and enjoy my tea for five minutes. A 4-year-old who has been exposed to the language of feelings can comprehend you, but a 2-year-old cannot. You are not saying, "You are annoying me, stop," or "You are acting badly." You are expressing your need for some time while feeling irritable and exhausted.

9. Other words of wisdom

Give yourself the same grace and forgiveness that you extend to your children, and give yourself as many chances to succeed as you do. Give yourself a loving hand. Your child will learn a valuable lesson from seeing that.

Aspect of Spirit, Soul and Body

This book has been setting out principles gained by studying what scientific research has to say. However, this is not the only aspect to consider when raising children.

All children and adults are created with a spirit, soul, and body, and each of these aspects of our being affects the other, within a person as a whole.

When we are born, our spirit is dead and we are cut off from a right relationship with our Creator who is perfect and righteous in all His ways.

This is a result of our sinful nature. The inherited sinful nature also affects our souls and body. We all know that we do not have to teach a child to do wrong, that comes easily. We have to work hard to teach them to do right, this is practical evidence of our sinful nature. That is not to say children, and adults, do not do what is right, not at all. We also do right because we were originally created in God's good image, but we are marred by sin.

Once we have recognized this, we realize why the 'Gospel' is Good News. You will find explained in the Gospels (Matthew, Mark, Luke, and John) in the Bible, the way that God has chosen to deal with our separation from Him and open the way back to a right relationship with Him. This then puts everything else in life into the right perspective.

It is simple but very profound, it is through Jesus Christ and His death on the cross – in our place, and His resurrection. So rather than just try and deal with one aspect of a child's being when raising them, why not address the whole of their being through Jesus Christ? Giving them the knowledge of the solid Rock of Jesus Christ whom they can choose to ask to be their Lord and Saviour would be the best foundation for life, and eternity, you could possibly give to your child, no matter their character and personality or where they live in the world.

May we invite you to investigate this further yourself by reading the Gospels. The New American Standard or the New King James are readily available. And here are a couple of helpful sites online:

https://livingwaters.com/are-you-a-good-person/

https://answersingenesis.org/bible/

Thanks Giving Note

Thanks for buying and reading our book, we hope you like our book, if you find it helpful and you like our content then give a review on our social media handles.

Please follow us for more updates about new amazing books and also follow us on our blog, website and on all social media platforms, links are available on our company's website. Visit and follow our website and blog (**www.fruitfulpublishers.com**) for monthly newsletters, weekly articles and amazing updates.

Regards

Fruitful Publishers

(UK Based Registered Publishing Company)

www.ingramcontent.com/pod-product-compliance
Lightning Source LLC
Chambersburg PA
CBHW042116100526
44587CB00025B/4081